Eugene C.

JoA
MANN

D0007985

THE FUNERAL AND THE MOURNERS

PAUL E. IRION

THE
FUNERAL
AND THE
MOURNERS

Pastoral Care of the Bereaved

Richmond Hill Library
2809 East Grace Street
Richmond, VA 23223

ABINGDON PRESS
New York   •   Nashville

03-195

THE FUNERAL AND THE MOURNERS

Copyright MCMLIV by Pierce & Washabaugh

All rights in this book are reserved.
No part of the book may be used or reproduced in
any manner whatsoever without written permission of
the publishers except brief quotations embodied in
critical articles or reviews. For information address
Abingdon Press, 810 Broadway, Nashville 2, Tennessee.

Library of Congress Catalog Card Number: 53-11337

SET UP, PRINTED, AND BOUND BY THE
PARTHENON PRESS, AT NASHVILLE,
TENNESSEE, UNITED STATES OF AMERICA

To
my father
ERNST FREDERICK IRION

who is now completing
nearly half a century
in the ministry of
the church

PREFACE

THE MYSTERY of death has always been surrounded, even in the most primitive cultures, by ritualistic forms. Because of the inexplicable quality of this event which draws the curtain on human existence, many cultures have seen a religious significance in it and have developed religious rites which are designed to interpret the meaning of death. These ceremonial acts are also a part of the pattern of disposing of the body of the deceased.

From very early times the Christian Church has conducted rites when death occurred in the fellowship. Inscriptions and drawings in the catacombs of Rome tell us that the primitive Church buried its dead with prayers and a service of Holy Communion. This simple ritual was elaborated upon during the ensuing centuries. By the age of the medieval Church the death and burial ritual had become the requiem mass. These rites have continued in their development to the present day with its highly stylized funeral service.

In recent years the funeral has been a very real concern to many pastors and congregations. Pamphlets and articles have been written calling for reforms in the funeral ritual and practices. Ministerial associations have engaged in campaigns to educate people in the true meaning of death and the attitude which Christian people should have toward it. Many of these efforts have achieved success in redirecting the pattern of the Protestant funeral service.

The discussion of the funeral in this book proposes reforms of ritual and practice, but they are of a different nature than the most widely published proposals of recent times. Many of the contemporary efforts at reform have been guided by theological, aesthetic, or economic considerations. These positions have been well taken,

7

because it is desirable that the funeral be theologically sound, aesthetically inoffensive, and that economic excesses be curtailed. However, it is the thesis of this volume that still another approach must be made to the funeral if it is to achieve its true significance in the lives of Christian people. The personal function of the funeral, what it does to and for the mourners, must be subjected to severe and critical evaluation and subsequent revision. We must establish more clearly the connection between the funeral and pastoral care.

The funeral has two aspects. On the one hand it is a service of divine worship conducted by the church in one of the crisis situations of life. It is a service in which man comes to God, bowed low, seeking the ever-present refuge and strength in time of trouble. All the common elements of Christian worship are contained in the funeral—praise, thanksgiving, supplication, and dedication. The funeral is divine worship. On the other hand the funeral has a personal function: it is designed and intended to do something for man. The Christian Church has never viewed worship as something which is entirely apart from human needs. It is focused upon God, to be sure; thereby it has meaning for the worshiper and his needs.

This volume limits itself to consideration of the personal function of the funeral. This is not a denial of the aspect of divine worship which is contained in the funeral ritual. Rather it is an attempt to show the way for the improvement of the means by which the funeral meets human needs, without in any sense detracting from the objective validity of the worship of God. This approach to the funeral is admittedly subjective, applying the principles which have been established through a psychological study of the grief reaction and mourning to the funeral ritual and practices as we know them.

The personal function of the funeral is seen as twofold: it is (1) to enable the individual to engage in the therapeutic process of mourning and (2) to present the Christian faith as a resource which makes it possible for him to enter this painful process not with trepidation, but with a sure and certain confidence that in mourning he will be comforted.

This project was undertaken after I had been serving as a parish minister for seven years. The seed of thought was planted on the day when, shortly after leaving the sanctuary of the seminary, I was called into a home where the father had that morning taken his own life. That seed has taken root and grown through countless pastoral calls and conversations with bereaved families. It has ripened to the conviction that a mere recitation of a ritual and conformity to accepted social patterns of mourning are not enough. Some effort must be made to improve the personal function of the funeral, to enable the pastor and the church to minister more effectively to those whose steps have taken them to the valley of the shadow of death. This book is the result of that conviction.

I have attempted to illustrate some points of this study with instances taken from my pastoral experience. Fictitious names are used, and in some cases the details of the situation have been altered, to preserve the anonymity of the individuals involved. Several cases are composites of the life experience of more than one person.

I am deeply indebted to the faculty of Eden Theological Seminary, Webster Groves, Missouri, for the grant of the Honor Graduate Fellowship which enabled me to pursue graduate studies in pastoral theology and counseling under the Federated Theological Faculty of the University of Chicago. My gratitude also goes to the congregation of Long Grove Church (Evangelical and Reformed) for the patience and forbearance with which they have accepted the part-time ministry that was necessitated by a schedule which divided the time of their pastor between the classroom and the parish. I am especially grateful to Seward Hiltner, Russell Becker, and Harold Wilke for the helpful comments and criticisms which they have contributed; to my wife, Mary Jean Irion, for the extra burden of parish work which she assumed in addition to the editing and typing of this manuscript; and to my son, Mark Stephen, for the co-operation of a four-year-old in accepting a moratorium on the pleasures of playing with his father.

Without these combined contributions my efforts to make this study would not have been possible.

PAUL IRION

CONTENTS

11

CHAPTER ONE

EXPLORING THE PROBLEM OF THE FUNERAL

THE MINISTRY of the church is defined by human need. Never in the history of the world has any institution been so concerned with meeting the needs of men. One of the most crucial of these arises in the experience of bereavement. The church must be there, standing ready to comfort the grief-stricken and to bind up the brokenhearted.

Death is the common lot of every man. John Donne wrote:

No man is an Iland, intire of it selfe; every man is a peece of the Continent, a part of the maine; if a Clod bee washed away by the Sea, Europe is the lesse, as well as if a Promontorie were, as well as if a Mannor of thy friends or of thine owne were; any mans death diminishes me, because I am involved in Mankinde; And therefore never send to know for whom the bell tolls; It tolls for thee.[1]

The great British poet-pastor voiced a real truth. The life of every man is so joined to the life of his fellow men that when one dies, a little of the life of all passes away. But we must recognize that in actual experience there are times when the tolling of the bell is too loud and too close, for death has touched the household or the circle of close friends. Then, the philosophical position of Donne notwithstanding, the feelings of the individual are much deeper and more moving. It is then that bereavement is experienced.

The universality of death has as its counterpart the universality of bereavement, which touches all classes, races, ages. Someone dies. That person has been an interactive part of the personal lives of a number of individuals. His activities and affections have been intermingled with those who live with and about him. As Donne

[1] *Devotions Upon Emergent Occasions*, XVII, "Meditation."

said, he is involved in the lives of his fellows. His death causes an interruption, a disintegration of the patterns of existence of those who knew him. Relationships are broken; activities are disrupted; friendships are severed. The person, his personality, his wants and needs, his contributions to the relationship, are lost. Those who remain are bereft; their loss is an experience of bereavement.

The acuteness of grief has attracted the interest and concern of students of the psyche who recognize the tremendous toll which it can exact from both the psyche and the soma. We now see that more than the physical presence of the deceased is lost. The whole system of meaningful relationships is also involved in the loss. When an aged grandmother dies, it is not just her presence in the home which is missed and the fact that her rocking chair is empty and her knitting needles are idle. But the warm milk that had to be prepared for her is no longer needed; the advice and counsel which she gave is no longer heard; the responsibility to keep one member of the family at home to care for her is unnecessary; the need for keeping the children quiet during her naptime is obviated. A whole new system of activities and relationships is brought about after Grandma's funeral. The survivors feel these changes in their pattern of life very keenly. It is part of their experience of bereavement. This situation can be the occasion for severe disintegration of the personality, or it can become a source of genuine strength. Some people may possess sufficient insight and resources to be able to come through the grief experience to a healthy adjustment to their loss. Others may find their lives so disrupted, their personalities so torn apart, that they are unable to re-establish a pattern of activity and relationships without the one who has died.

From the very beginning the church has felt a responsibility to minister to the grief-stricken, to provide aid and comfort for them in their bereavement. The early church fathers wrote letters of consolation to those in the fellowship who had suffered the loss of a loved one.[2] They attempted to give comfort by assuring the

[2] Cf. J. T. McNeill, *A History of the Cure of Souls* (New York: Harper & Bros., 1951), pp. 102 ff.

mourners and reminding them of the Christian view of death and resurrection.

In the established patterns of Western culture the church is almost always present in the grief situation. For some this may be due to the fact that it is the accepted thing to do: a death requires a funeral; a funeral requires the church. This is seen in its extreme form in the growing practice in some metropolitan areas for the funeral service to be conducted by a clergyman who is hired by the undertaker, without being attended by any of the family. For some it may be motivated by a genuine reliance upon the spiritual foundation of their lives and their desire to receive the comfort of the Christian fellowship in their hour of need. For others it may be a quasi superstition in the face of the mystery of death, a force which is relentless even in the age of scientific medicine, a phenomenon which defies explanation and understanding. Hence religion seems to be the logical place from which to seek help. But no matter whether the church is called upon because of tradition and custom, faith and fellowship, or superstition and fear, the church does enter into almost every experience of bereavement.

For these reasons the treatment of bereavement is one of the few areas of life which is still largely in the hands of the church. The responsibility for education, charity, moral regulation, and cultural development has been relegated largely to other social agencies. But the care of the bereaved has not been taken from the church. Every pastor still has the opportunity to minister to those who have suffered loss by death, even though he no longer is called upon to educate the children of the parish in parochial schools, distribute food to the needy, care for the orphans, preserve law and order in the community, or provide the only community cultural outlet in the music and art of the church. Therefore it is essential that the minister prepare himself for the ministry to the bereaved.

The church has not been unaware of this obligation. It has sought to minister to the grief-stricken in manifold ways. There have been efforts to make an educational preparation for death and bereavement in sermons and printed statements about the Christian position on death, burial customs, and so on. These efforts have been designed to stimulate the thinking of people in objective situations rather than in the presence of death. Certainly a great deal of good can be accomplished by such an educational effort. The church also ministers to the bereaved in the funeral service in which there are both the witness to the Christian hope and a sympathetic understanding of the feelings of the mourners. The funeral is a service which marks the termination of an earthly life, a means of providing sympathy and support through the community of the Christian fellowship, and an endeavor to determine and meet the individual needs of the mourners. A third way in which the church has sought to provide help to the grief-stricken may be called postfuneral counseling. This may be seen in the letters of consolation written by the early church fathers, in the pastoral calls which have been made in homes of sorrow by faithful pastors, in the contemporary endeavors of some ministers to bring psychological knowledge to bear by counseling with the bereaved for weeks, and months if need be, to enable them to assimilate the experience of their sorrow. The church has not been unmindful of the tremendous responsibility which it has in this sensitive area in the lives of men.

The awakening of ministers to the aid which can be derived from the work of modern dynamic psychology is a crucial point in the treatment of bereavement in any of the ways described above. The dynamic understanding of grief will be described in detail in Chapter II, but here I wish to indicate that the psychological knowledge which we now have directs us away from the "traditional" treatment of bereavement to a new therapy, which is proven helpful and effective. I shall treat this much more explicitly later, but for the sake of illustration let us compare the two approaches in a characterization of two types of contemporary ministers.

Pastor A., who represents the classical method, is called to the home of a bereaved family. He is a sensitive man who feels the joys and sorrows of his people keenly. As he talks with the grieving husband and father, he feels the burden of suffering and loss. Partly because this situation pains him and partly because he senses the painfulness of the experience to his parishioner, he seeks to bring comfort which will relieve the pain. In his prefuneral and postfuneral ministry to this family he will search his spiritual resources for those elements which he feels will assuage the pain. Pastor A. seeks to apply the comfort of Scripture, Christian peace and hope, to these friends as a means for sustaining them in their hour of trial. But his efforts are designed toward one end, the displacement of their grief by faith and hope. If they can only use this grievous experience to support and strengthen their faith, the sorrow which assails them will be eased and disappear. We might say that this approach is designed as a displacement or sublimation of grief by fostering the growth of faith and hope, thereby giving comfort.

Pastor B. is also very much concerned for the well-being of his parishioners. Called into the home of a bereaved family, he too feels very deeply the loss which they are experiencing. He too draws heavily upon the promises of the Word, the faith and hope which are in the heart of the Christian. But his intention is quite different from that of Pastor A. He realizes that comfort is not a substitute or replacement for mourning, that one does not remove mourning by putting a double portion of comfort in its place. Rather he sees that as we mourn, we are comforted. Basing his ministry on the spiritual resources which he has as a Christian pastor and his knowledge of dynamic psychology, he sees that the painful work of mourning must be gone through before comfort can truly come. Therefore his approach is to strengthen people for mourning rather than to assist them in escaping from it.

In these very brief and obviously incomplete characterizations we see the key to the change which has been made by the impact of dynamic psychology in ministering to the bereaved. It is upon this crucial fact that this study hinges.

Although there is a real need for studying and interpreting the church's whole ministry to the grief-stricken—the educational preparation for death and bereavement, the funeral service and the practices which attend it, and postfuneral counseling—I shall address my attention only to the second aspect, the funeral. Not every pastor seeks avenues through sermons and pastoral letters for preparing his people for the day when death comes close to them. Not every pastor feels capable of counseling with the bereaved in the difficult time after the funeral. But every pastor is called upon to conduct funeral services for members of his church and community. Thus it seems both logical and expedient to focus our attention on that phase of the ministry to those who mourn which is common to all ministers—the funeral.

Extensive studies of the funeral have been made from the standpoint of both the traditional and the theological aspects of funeral practices. There are a number of resource books for pastors which will assist them in understanding the meaning and rationale behind many of the customs and practices which make up our funerals. There are other volumes which deal with the theological implications of the funeral ritual, the Christian view of death applied to funeral practices. But there is a great need for studying the funeral service in its psychological dimension, framed by the needs of the individual mourner. It is this task which I undertake here.

The actual service and ritual can be seen in this respect to have several functions. It is a means of establishing rapport between the pastor and the grief-stricken. It offers the pastor a unique opportunity to demonstrate the acuity of his understanding of the feelings of the mourners as they go through the spiritual and emotional experience which we call the funeral. It also gives the pastor an opportunity to interpret properly the meaning of the impact of death and bereavement. The minister employs both his theological interpretation and his psychological knowledge in understanding the experiences and feelings of the mourners. In like manner the funeral service provides the pastor with an opportunity for opening the beginning phases of the process of aiding the person toward an adjustment and reintegration of his life. The minister's conduct of the funeral service not only illuminates the depth of his own understanding of the problem but also establishes the climate in which postfuneral counseling can grow into a fruitful experience.

An analysis of the funeral service from the point of view of religious psychology is pertinent in three ways. It is of importance for the study of pastoral psychology. This field is of such recent vintage that it seeks exhaustive examination in all phases of the ministry to individuals. Its coverage of the vital material has been limited, not by the lack of ability of its students nor the paucity of phenomena to be studied, but by the sheer lack of time for an adequate study of the many phases of its concern. Very little has been written about the ministry to the bereaved from the standpoint of dynamic psychology. Many other virgin fields could be enumerated. A study of the psychological dimension of the funeral service can be helpful to the field of pastoral psychology by indicating ways in which the funeral ritual is a phase of precounseling activity which opens the way, or closes it, to the opportunities of the minister to counsel with the bereaved.

The study of the funeral is also important for the parishioners of the church. The adage first spoken by Benjamin Franklin that "in this world nothing is certain but death and taxes" might be augmented by the word "grief." The life of the average individual will inevitably be touched by an experience of bereavement. Thus any endeavor to make of the funeral service an occasion for receiving the help which is actually needed by the parishioner should be of positive consequence to him.

The study of the funeral from a psychological viewpoint is also pertinent to the church and the minister. The church has traditionally accepted as part of its task the injunction, "Comfort ye my people." Throughout the centuries the church and ministry have dedicated themselves to this task. While "to comfort" originally meant "to strengthen," it gradually came to connote giving relief from suffering. Christian comfort lost in part the recognition of the faith as a source of strength in tribulation and made of it a mere placebo. Now through an understanding of the dynamic forces operative in the life of the individual, the church is becoming increasingly aware of a new potentiality for the accomplishment and fulfillment of one of its commissions.

The problem then is to examine the funeral ritual and practices which are in current use, to evaluate them in the psychological dimension, and to arrive at general principles which will be helpful in the formulation and interpretation of funeral practices of constructive value for the church, its pastors and parishioners.

CHAPTER TWO

BEREAVEMENT IN THE LIGHT OF PSYCHOLOGY

THE INTERRELATIONSHIP of psychology and religion is an alliance of long standing. Generically both disciplines pertain to the study and examination of the psyche, the soul. For many centuries the only concern for the spirit of man was held by those whose interest and work were primarily religious. However, there was seldom any concerted effort to make this psychology explicit as such. Consequently psychological studies were considered tangential to the literature of the theological discipline.

When secular science gradually reduced its focus from the cosmos to the world, from the world to the body of man, from man's body to his mind and spirit, it took the study of psychology out of the pale of religion. In a sense this was due to the fact that religious thinking was too preoccupied with traditional theological problems to see the benefits which would accrue from a scientific appraisal of the nature of man. Unfortunately, however, psychology became a science at the time when science was looked upon as an antagonist of religion. It was the old story of Galileo and Copernicus with a variation only in the stage setting. Psychology joined with the other sciences in attacking the defensive, *status quo* attitude of religion. Some of the early proponents of the scientific study of the psyche added their voices and pens to the denunciation of religion as an illusion and a source of neuroses. These attacks from both sides delayed a reconciliation for several decades. Only as a *rapprochement* was reached between the sciences of man and theological disciplines, a relatively recent development, has psychology regained a useful status in Christian thinking and endeavor. We now see the contribution to the understanding of man and his whole existence, physical and spiritual, which can be made by the co-operative endeavors of a reconciled science and religion.

Although secular psychology developed rapidly, a few religious scholars were beginning to awaken to the way in which it could be of service. Men like William James and Edwin Starbuck began to study and interpret religious experience in the light of the findings of psychology. Others, like Anton Boisen, saw the relationship of religion and its resources to mental illness and health. The reconciliation was begun.

The work of psychology had not been static during this period. It passed through the phases of faculty psychology and behaviorism. It learned from the work of Freud and psychoanalysis. It came to a dynamic understanding of the human personality. This dynamic psychology opened the door for a new and fruitful approach to the work of the church and to pastoral care and counseling. "The kind of psychological understanding which is relevant to pastoral counseling is a social psychology of personality in movement, moving and being moved, motivating and being motivated, operating as a unit on a human social level as well as on other levels such as the biological." [1] Pastoral work has always been individualistic. It has been concerned with the welfare of the individual spirit—the cure of the individual soul. Although the pastor works with his entire congregation, his real impact is felt upon individual lives. Dynamic psychology has brought a new individualism to the fore. It sees the person living, not in isolation, but in a network of interpersonal relationships. The individual is still the focal point, but viewed against a field of all the personalities surrounding him. The feeling, motivation, self-concept, of the individual are determined and influenced by the two-way relationships which he maintains with other people.

Seward Hiltner has summarized the implications which dynamic psychology offers for pastoral work.[2] Dynamic psychology has demonstrated that human conduct cannot be viewed as superficial. There is a depth dimension which must be taken into account.

[1] Seward Hiltner, *Pastoral Counseling* (New York and Nashville: Abingdon-Cokesbury Press, 1949), p. 56.
[2] *Ibid.*, pp. 71-79.

Every action carries with it a residue of meaning which can be understood only by appreciating the depth factor. While we may view a person's conduct horizontally, that is, spread upon the surface of life, we can never understand it until we see it vertically as well, reaching back into the inner feelings and motivations of the individual. This should not be interpreted to indicate that the person himself always understands what his actions mean. More often than not, the depth dimension of behavior is wholly unconscious. Both aspects, the conscious and the unconscious, must be taken into account to understand truly the individual and his behavior. Another pertinent implication which is raised by dynamic psychology is that the human personality grows not by avoiding conflict or seeking to escape from it, but by handling the conflicts of life positively and constructively. Even the most naïve would have to admit to the presence of conflict in human life. Tensions and pressures are present inside and outside every life. Dynamic psychology has said that therapy does not consist of walling the individual off from his conflicts nor opening the gate for a hasty retreat; true therapy enables the individual to recognize and face the conflicting issues and tensions of life, take the leap of faith and struggle through them. Dealing with the conflicts of life constructively provides both the insights and the resources for further growth. One other implication of dynamic psychology assumes that within the individual is a force or power which enables him to meet and act upon the conflicts of life. This is not something which the pastor or therapist provides for or induces into the person. Rather it can be seen as the creative spirit of God operative in his creation. This power within the individual is the key to the appropriation of dynamic psychology into the work of the Christian church and pastor.

As we apply these implications of dynamic psychology to the grief situation, we immensely deepen our understanding of what goes on in the life and personality of the bereaved. Only the bold outline of this application is stated here because it is the foundation upon which the ministry to the grief-stricken is based. Its wider meaning and application will be dealt with more fully later.

In the first place, when we see the meaningfulness of life described in terms of interpersonal relationships, we recognize that the life of every individual is in part determined by, even made up of, the lives of other individuals, When one life is removed by death, it causes a disruption of a complex web of relationships. The amount and depth of the interaction seem to bear a direct relationship to the depth and scope of the grief reaction.

Secondly, the fact of the depth dimension of human behavior aids our ability to understand the great variety of reactions which are manifested in the bereaved. We see that the behavior of the mourner not only is a manifestation of a sense of loss or deprivation but may reflect a multitude of other feelings which have their roots deep within the unconsciousness of the person. This would lead one to assume that the understanding of a person's grief is inevitably accompanied by a concommitant understanding of the person himself.

Thirdly, we recognize that the therapy for bereavement does not involve a denial of the tensions and inner conflicts which are involved nor an escape from them. Genuine therapy results only when there is a constructive assimilation of and adjustment to these conflicts—working them through, fighting them out, building on their breached and fallen walls.

In the fourth place, we are guided and encouraged by the fact that there is within the individual a creative spirit, the spirit of God, which makes such therapeutic action possible. The work of the church and the pastor is to provide the climate in which that spirit can exert itself. The ministry to the bereaved is dedicated to that end.

Psychological Studies of Bereavement

This understanding of bereavement was not arrived at in one stroke of insight. It is the cumulative result of the work of several physicians of the spirit. A brief survey of their writings will give us the outline of their positions, the major thrust of their work, and the unique contributions which were made by each. The data and implications of their studies will be included in the more comprehensive description of grief.

The first modern interest in a study of bereavement was shown by Sigmund Freud.[3] He saw a great similarity between people who were in mourning and the melancholics who came to the psychoanalyst. Both were undergoing many of the same reactions: terrible dejection, loss of interest in the real outside world, a loss of the capacity to love, an inhibitive curtailment of meaningful activity, feelings of self-reproach which eventuate in a feeling of being punished or the expectation of punishment. Freud made his original contribution in this delineation of the variety of feelings which compose bereavement, showing them to be vastly more involved than mere sadness because of loss. His explanation gives rise to the possibility of a dynamic understanding of the many forces and pressures which complicate the lives of the mourner.

Defining mourning as the reaction to the loss of a loved one, Freud recognized that there was a certain residue left in the life of the mourner by the deceased. The fact that the person was gone physically did not mean that he was not still present in the emotions of the mourner. The tension between the real physical absence and the just as real mental or emotional presence brings about a serious disturbance in the life of the mourner. The meaningfulness of the outside world is not appreciated, except as it recalls the deceased. Thus there can be no capacity for love because this would mean seeking a new love which would replace the one who is mourned. This disturbance becomes so pronounced that it constitutes a very painful experience for the bereaved.

Freud's therapy for mourners grows out of this understanding of the experience of grief.

The struggle can be so intense that a turning away from reality ensues, the object being clung to through the medium of a hallucinatory wish-psychosis. The normal outcome is that deference for reality gains the day.

[3] "Mourning and Melancholia," *Collected Papers*, The International Psycho-analytical Library (London: Hogarth Press and Institute of Psycho-Analysis, 1948), IV, 152-70.

Nevertheless its behest cannot be at once obeyed. The task is now carried through bit by bit, under great expense of time and cathectic energy, while all the time the existence of the lost object is continued in the mind. Each single one of the memories and hopes which bound the libido to the object is brought up and hypercathected, and the detachment of the libido from it is accomplished.[4]

By this Freud is saying that the attachment of the libido of the mourner to the deceased is painfully and gradually broken in the process of mourning. It is a necessary process because without it the individual will remain inhibited and out of touch with reality. Unless mourning is done, and done properly, the libido remains attached to the lost love object and is thwarted in any possible opportunity to grow. Only by continual testing of reality, affirming constantly the fact that the loved one is gone, can the libido be detached and a new integration made.

In this Freud made a very positive contribution to the understanding of bereavement. He recognized in his own particular way the interpersonal aspect of which I have spoken. However, his theory lends itself only to what might be called a positive attachment, a love relationship. The theory would not be applicable to the grief reaction in a situation of negative attachment, where hostility rather than love characterized the relationship.

Melanie Klein continued this line of reasoning, speaking of mourning as grief work. The bereaved had to go over and over memories which surrounded the deceased until he was sufficiently emancipated to assume new relationships. Only then would life resume a normal pattern.

The most outstanding study of grief in modern psychiatry is the work of Erich Lindemann.[5] His work is supported by a number of case studies of individuals who are bereaved. A large portion of this study, which substantiated earlier investigation, was conducted among survivors of the disastrous Cocoanut Grove fire in Boston. By working with the hospitalized victims of the tragedy, many of whom had lost friends or relatives in the fire, the psy-

[4] Ibid., p. 154. Used by permission of the publisher.
[5] "Symptomatology and Management of Acute Grief," The American Journal of Psychiatry, Sept., 1944, pp. 141-49.

chiatrist and his aides were able to draw and to support a number of interesting conclusions. It was shown that there is a definite syndrome, that is, a common pattern of symptoms and reactions experienced by individuals in acute grief. It was demonstrated that this syndrome did not necessarily appear immediately following the death. It could be repressed or delayed, giving the impression that it did not exist in a particular individual. In some people the syndrome could assume inappropriate and distorted variations.

The syndrome which Lindemann described contains the following reactions which are common to individuals experiencing acute grief. There are physical sensations such as tightness in the throat, choking, shortness of breath, a need for sighing, an empty feeling in the abdomen, feelings of muscular weakness, and feelings of painful inner tension. These sensations tend to come in waves which are stimulated by experiences such as meeting a sympathizing friend, an object or remark which summons forth a memory of the deceased, or a demonstration of kindness which recalls the loss. The minister who works with the bereaved members of his parish is undoubtedly familiar with these symptoms of the grief reaction.

The significance of Lindemann's explanation of the syndrome is not merely the value of the factual description nor the clear demonstration of the painfulness of the experience. The true significance is also to be found in the use of this symptomatic pattern as a means for understanding the grief experience, as an evaluative tool in gauging its severity, and as a detector of the presence of morbid or distorted reactions.

The therapy for bereavement which Lindemann suggests begins where Freud stopped. Lindemann recognizes that there is a direct correlation between the degree of interaction of the mourner and the deceased and the severity of the grief reaction. But he would not limit the interaction to a positive or affectionate relationship. The same severity of reaction could be found in a situation where there was a negative attachment, an interaction characterized by hostility or resentment.

The mourning process is once again interpreted as an emancipation from the bondage to the deceased, a reintegration of life within the framework of an environment from which the deceased has gone, and the establishment of new interpersonal relationships. It becomes a process of reliving certain areas of life, recalling memories of the past, thinking freely of the deceased, and honestly facing up to the adjustments which are now necessary. This process is difficult because it is painful. The mourning process is one of suffering, but it is therapeutic suffering. As the process continues, there is a gradual release from the tension and distress which formerly were so painful. Lindemann's therapy is not so much a deliberate severing of attachments as an assimilation of the experience of living with the memory of the deceased, yet not in bondage to it.

The work of William F. Rogers[6] has taken the findings of these psychological studies of the grief reactions and translated them into concrete applications for the work of the ministry. The interpretation of the psychological data concerning grief and mourning in the light of Christian doctrine and spiritual resources is extremely helpful to the pastor. The work of Rogers forms the bridge which aids the study of any aspect of bereavement from the standpoint of the ministry of the church. The brevity with which I deal with Rogers at this point is by no means an indication that his work is of small consequence. Quite the contrary, it is the most fruitful book which has been written in the field for the pastor. A considerable portion of the interpretation of the meaning and content of grief which will be presented below is based upon Rogers' observations.

Insights Gained from Psychological Studies of Bereavement

From these very cursory descriptions of the psychological studies of grief which have been made we gain a number of insights: (1) we do find that there are resources of personality to meet the impact of grief without the benefit of help from a clergyman; (2) the grief reaction is potentially more complex than is commonly imagined; (3) there are distorted reaction patterns which some-

* *Ye Shall Be Comforted.*

times arise; (4) mourning, properly understood, is a therapeutic experience. The first three of these insights need not be explicated in great detail at this point, but we must see the basic framework of their subject matter in order to formulate the rationale for the fourth insight, which is crucial to this study of the funeral.

The first insight which is achieved through a psychological understanding of the grief reaction is that there are resources of personality within the individual which, if properly used, enable the bereaved to withstand the weight of grief. The implication is that therapy does not come about through any activity of the minister which is designed to supply or add strength from the outside of the mourner. Personality itself has the power to react with or without the ministry of the church. However, this does not obviate entirely the work of the minister in the grief situation. The function of the pastor, or counselor, or friend is to open the way and to prepare a favorable environment for the inner resources of the mourner to meet his needs.

The second proposition is that grief is primarily an emotion, or more accurately, a complex of feelings. Modern psychological studies have shown that feelings of guilt, hostility, fear, bewilderment, and loneliness often accompany the feeling of sorrow which we recognize as a characteristic of bereavement. So often in the past only the positive feeling of sorrow because of loss has been recognized and associated with grief. Now we see that there is also the possibility that powerful negative feelings, such as hostility and guilt, are very much a part of the grief reaction. As W. Barnett Blakemore stated:

An important part of the recent grief studies is that the extent and depth of grief tends to be directly dependent upon the amount and depth of interaction, either positive or negative, that has existed between the bereaved and the deceased. The fact that this may be either positive or negative has shed light on some phenomena which previously seemed irrational.[7]

[7] "Funerals in the Light of Our Knowledge of Grief and Bereavement," Summarized Report of Joint Session of May 5, 1950, Department of Pastoral Services, Commission on Religion and Health, Federal Council of Churches.

We know that emotional tensions within the individual not only create psychic pressures but also set off a chain reaction in the body. Disturbances of the functioning of the endocrine glands create a call for muscular and neural action. This chain of events demands some type of responsive action. "Emotion requires action. Love requires the expression of affection; anger requires attack; and fear requires flight. . . . Grief is an acute, and a difficult, emotion to deal with because of the inability to do anything about the loss which has brought it on." [8]

However, since grief is an extremely painful emotion, and especially since it is often accompanied by the even more excruciating negative feelings toward the deceased and the self, grief is denied or delayed. This is essentially a mechanism to escape the painfulness of the situation. There are a number of ways in which the individual can seemingly avoid or dispose of grief by forcing it out of consciousness. There may be involved effort to rationalize the situation, extreme self-control to avoid any of the physical symptoms described by Lindemann, concentrated efforts to find new interests, to avoid loneliness and to prevent the mind from thinking about the deceased. All of these are devices for avoiding the feeling which we commonly call grief.

Dynamic psychology has demonstrated that there are resources within man and available to him which enable him to recover from traumatic experiences such as bereavement. Most grief reactions will eventually diminish in severity by themselves. This does not mean that a pastor or counselor cannot function as a catalyst to speed the working of the mourning process and to decrease the possibility of a preliminary period of repression.

Psychological studies, from Freud to modern times, demonstrate very clearly that merely forcing a fact or feeling out of consciousness by no means destroys or removes it. Repressed emotions can build to volcanic proportions as they are kept beneath the surface of consciousness. When eruption finally occurs, the consequences are much more severe than they would have been had the original feeling been dealt with by confrontation and assimila-

[8] Rogers, *op. cit.*, p. 20.

tion rather than by repression. Repression not only drives feelings out of consciousness but also necessitates a system of defenses against their recurrence in consciousness. The progressive thickening of this armor plate makes the passage of thoughts and feelings from unconsciousness into consciousness more difficult and more painful.

The third insight gained from psychological studies describes morbid or distorted grief reactions. Very often in the past the cause of death, the manner of death, the time of death, have been considered to be determining influences in the degree or type of reaction which is experienced. Now we have come to see that the fundamental structure of the personality of the mourner is crucial to the extent and kind of grief reaction. We know that loss through death brings a disruption of the pattern of the personal activities of the mourner and a dislocation of certain elements of the role of the self. If the personhood of the mourner is already somewhat disintegrated, a severe distortion is likely to take place in bereavement attitudes and conduct. These morbid reactions vary in severity in direct proportion to the lack of integration within the individual.

The work of Lindemann describes nine distorted reactions which are seen as deviations from the normal behavior patterns of the individual brought on by experiences of acute grief. (1) There may be a burst of energy and enthusiasm which is quite uncharacteristic for the person. He may plunge into new tasks or activities without indicating any sense of loss or deprivation. (2) There may be in other individuals a reaction which goes to the opposite extreme. Where once the person was capable of normal social relationships, he may now withdraw from any interaction. This does not mean that he necessarily becomes a hermit, but it indicates that he now lacks those qualities which make social relationships possible. He takes no initiative in friendship, is indecisive and unwilling to accept social responsibility. (3) Closely akin to this is a growing social isolation from friends or members of the family. The once sweet-tempered individual may become volatile and irritable. (4) Some people begin to demonstrate terrific hostility. Very often this takes the form of blaming someone for the death. The family doctor, close relatives, persons who are innocently involved in an accident fatal to the deceased, are frequent targets for such hostility. (5) In some individuals the hostility becomes so acute and so unexpressible that it gives rise to a schizophrenic condition. (6) There are some people who become involved in various activities which are completely out of character and which place a serious strain on their social or economic wellbeing. They may, for example, become generous to the point of poor judgment, unconsciously punishing themselves by sacrificing their possessions. (7) Certain psychosomatic illnesses appear to have a definite relationship to distorted grief reactions. Most common among them are rheumatoid arthritis, ulcerated colitis, and asthma. (8) There are instances in which the bereaved begins to assume symptoms which are characteristic of the disease from which the deceased suffered. (9) Extreme and agitated depression can be observed in some individuals. The person becomes convinced of his own worthlessness, is restless and wrought up, is filled with self-recrimination and a morbid desire to be punished.

While these reactions are recognized to be severe, we should not be led to imagine that they are uncommon. Every pastor, equipped with the proper diagnostic tools and insight, would be able to see a number of these reactions among his parishioners. Most often they occur in those individuals who have repressed or delayed their grief rather than letting it come to the surface and working through it immediately following their loss.

For this reason the work of mourning assumes primary importance when we deal with the grief situation. Mourning brings comfort because it provides release from the pain which accompanies bereavement.

Even the brief survey of the psychological data on grief which I have made should indicate the potency and violence of grief. It is like a terrible disease which attacks both body and spirit. The longer it is permitted to work its destruction, the greater toll it takes. If the work of mourning is not done within several months, there may be lasting devastation in the life of the individual.

Freud in comparing melancholia with mourning wrote:

Mourning is regularly the reaction to the loss of a loved person. . . . Although grief involves great departures from the normal attitude of life, it never occurs to us to regard it as a morbid condition and hand the mourner over to medical treatment. We rest assured that after a lapse of time it will be overcome, and we look upon any interference with it as inadvisable or even harmful.[9]

While Freud did not have the benefit of Lindemann's discoveries of delayed and distorted grief reactions, the basic thrust of his statement is still true. If the person is willing to do the work of mourning, there will be relief and release from the bondage to grief.

In a way the medical profession does a disservice to so many people when death occurs in the family. The indiscriminate use of sedation for the bereaved shortly after the death is not doing them a favor by sparing them pain, unless, of course, some physical condition makes such a traumatic experience dangerous. So often sedation only delays the reaction until the person gets away from the doctor or hospital chaplain. Then the reaction hits with full fury, but now there is no professional assistance to direct the impact into therapeutic channels.

While I would not say that it is the function of the pastor and counselor to induce mourning in his parishioner, the pastor must guard against doing anything which circumvents or discourages the work of mourning. In this respect a statement of the psychological meaning and benefit of mourning is pertinent to this study.

It is essential that grief be confronted squarely. The bereaved must be willing to admit that grief is present, recognizing it and accepting it as a very real force in life. Any attempt to sublimate it or deny its existence guarantees its continuance and precludes any effort to deal with it. Mourning, painful though it is, has to be faced if comfort is to follow. The human animal instinctively avoids pain. Nevertheless experience illustrates that there are those times when pain has value, not only as a sign that something is

[9] *Op. Cit.*, p. 153.

wrong, but also as a necessary accompaniment of healing. The pain
of an aching tooth may be temporarily avoided by "getting your
mind off it" or by taking an aspirin to deaden it, but in order
to bring about permanent relief, the diseased molar must be ex-
tracted, an experience which is psychically, if not physically,
painful. One may temporarily avoid the pain of grief by refusing
to admit the loss, by refusing to think about the deceased, by
doing a hundred and one things to keep the mind occupied with
happier thoughts, by bizarre attempts to keep the illusion of the
loved one alive; but any relief which may come will not be lasting.
There is no reality to sustain such devices. They only serve to
push grief deeper into the unconscious, where it becomes increasingly potent, capable of terrible destruction in the life of the
individual.

The fourth insight which we gain from the psychological
studies of grief has to do with the beneficial nature of mourning.
The therapy of mourning might be thought of as having two
major parts: accepting memories of the deceased and sharing the
grief work by social interaction.

From the time of Freud's theory of libido detachment to the
work of Lindemann and Rogers there is recognition of the necessity
for learning to live with the memories of the deceased. We know
that these memories bring about painful reactions. The syndrome
of grief is set in motion by objects or words which remind the
bereaved of the deceased. In the early stages of mourning actual
physical and emotional discomforts are induced by such memories.
But as time passes and the remembered image of the deceased is
confronted, thought about, talked about, the pain gradually les-
sens and an adjustment to further memories is possible.

We must bear in mind that when we speak of memories of the
deceased, we are not necessarily assuming that these are pleasant
memories of loving and affectionate association. There is also the
presence of unpleasant memories, of dislikes and disagreements, of
resentment, possibly even hatred. These unpleasant memories and
the negative feelings which they call to mind must be faced and
scrutinized and discussed. Until the mourner is able to live with

the image of the deceased with all its positive or negative connotations, the image will persist and the painful experience of grief will continue.

Here then is the first therapeutic activity: memories of the deceased must be accepted.

The second step of the therapy of mourning draws heavily from the development of psychotherapy. After the mourner has begun the extremely painful work of recalling memories of the deceased and accepting them, there is a need to talk about them. This talking process has a triple therapeutic value. In the first place, it is cathartic. As the experience is discussed over and over, its painfulness is gradually lessened and relieved. It has already been stated that the inner tensions which are built up in the grief experience demand release. Action is required to relieve the tension. Just as an angry man yells and a terrified woman screams, a bereaved individual may find release in talking. The deep feelings of loss, of lostness, of loneliness, of guilt or resentment, are brought closer to the surface where they can be dealt with; and the tension level decreases.

In the second place, the talking process provides important insights for the individual himself. The real feelings and problems which are troubling the parishioner are seen more clearly. As they are dealt with, new feelings and reactions are forthcoming. This is the positive complement to the cathartic aspect of the talking.

In the third place, the talking process establishes a relationship which is supportive. This does not mean that the pastor places himself in a position where the mourner may become overly dependent on him. Rather it means that the relationship is characterized by an attitude of empathy, a deep feeling of the problem. In a sense the minister shares the work of mourning with the individual. He indicates his very real concern for the person's well-being. He often partially fills the vacuum of loneliness which accompanies bereavement.

There is genuine religious significance in this psychological explanation of the therapy of mourning. In the Christian faith we find the resources for implementing the therapy. We see that re-

ligion is not to be looked upon as a substitute for grief. Faith is
not a means for short-circuiting mourning. Rather in the Christian
faith we find the strength and resources which enable us to face
and pass through the painful experience of mourning.

The Christian faith, seen in its true meaning, gives every
justification for mourning. The belief in the working of the Spirit
of God in the lives of men, strengthening and sustaining them in
crises, enriches the psychologist's faith in a power for health which
resides in man. This belief enables man to entrust himself to the
therapeutic process of mourning, which is a means to health. The
strength to bring him to reintegration will be there if he is willing
to trust himself to the process. In similar fashion the Christian belief in the value of confession and the forgiveness of sins enables the
mourner to enter the process without trepidation, without fearing
feelings of guilt or indications of failure which may come out in
rigorous self-examination. Then, too, the new integration of life
without the deceased can be faced in confidence, because the Christian faith of the individual provides him with a system of values
and a purpose for living which neither abrogate his feelings for
the deceased nor make him inordinately dependent upon them.

Unfortunately the church often abets the delay of the grief
reaction and thwarts the therapeutic process. In our desire to be
of help and comfort we unconsciously give people the idea that
expression of grief betrays a lack of faith. The church has often
been guilty of misinterpreting the words of the apostle, "But we
would not have you ignorant, brethren, concerning those who
are asleep, that you may not grieve as others do who have no
hope" (I Thess. 4:13 R.S.V.). Failing to appreciate the true meaning of these words, the church has given grief the connotation of
wrongness and apostasy. It is reasoned that belief in immortality
should enable a person to control his grief and sublimate his mourning. So good Christian people, believing in life everlasting, feeling
that they must not allow what they really feel to come to the
surface lest they be untrue to their faith, repress and suppress their
grief. It is true that faith in the life everlasting is a comfort when
one is concerned with the spiritual welfare of the deceased. But

it says nothing to deny the deep sense of loss which has been suffered. It is entirely legitimate and consistent with the Christian position to mourn, to feel and express grief because of loss and separation and loneliness, confident that it is a part of the therapeutic process.

Just as the church sometimes wrongly harms the individual by misinterpreting the real meaning of mourning, so, too, the mores apply pressures which thwart the therapy of mourning. Most cultures have a highly developed pattern which reactions of grief should follow. There are established duties required of mourners. Some cultures have even developed a class of professional mourners who excel in the performance of these obligations to custom. Our own culture has a prescribed pattern for formal mourning, which is observed in varying degree from one community to another. There are required forms of dress symbolic of the feelings which the person should be having. There are restricted social activities. There is the requirement for the "proper amount of tears" to demonstrate affection for the deceased, but yet the need to "bear up wonderfully." In all these ways the outward show of grief is limited and formed by socially prescribed patterns, with little regard for what the mourner actually feels.

Most cultures also have strong taboos involving death which color the mourning patterns—for example, the euphemism designed to mask the stark reality of death. We refer to someone "passing away"; we refer to the deceased as "asleep" or "departed." Extreme forms of the euphemistic treatment of death form the core of a very interesting satirical novelette, *The Loved One* by Evelyn Waugh,[10] in which he describes the epitome of disguising death by the plushy mortician's artistry. Such taboos reflect the desire to treat death as something unreal, as if one could deaden the pain of loss by denying its reality. Naturally this creates a terrific conflict within the individual mourner. He knows the reality of the loss as no one else can possibly know it. Yet all around him the culture and his social group are doing everything possible to deny or disguise it.

[10] Boston: Little, Brown & Co., 1948.

The cultural forces exert their pressures in a way which amounts to the loss of freedom by the individual. He is not free to act in accordance with his real feelings. He must express the feelings, and only those feelings, which are socially acceptable.

The bereaved are surrounded by friends who attempt to keep their minds occupied with pleasant thoughts. They receive a flood of advice and exhortation to be brave and composed. Unfortunately most of this goes under the guise of comfort when in reality it is a hindrance to real comfort.

The culture may demand a show of emotion to prove affection. There is certain to be comment about a wife who goes through the entire period of her husband's death and burial without shedding a single tear. Her devotion or fidelity will be questioned. Thus it is conceivable that an individual could be forced into a pseudo grief reaction which does not allow a genuine release of emotion. Concommitantly feelings of guilt and hostility would corrode the personality, making an honest integration virtually impossible.

Or the culture may demand stringent emotional control, not allowing the person to give vent to his feelings. A man may feel compelled to control his emotions to demonstrate the courage of his manhood. Or a misinterpretation of the meaning and intention of the Christian faith regarding death, as described above, may lead a person to avoid mourning.

Two apparently contradictory ideas have been expressed here: that the culture sometimes prescribes that a "proper amount of grief" be shown to demonstrate affection, and that grief be controlled to demonstrate poise, courage, or faith. While the reactions may be quite different, in both the culture demands a certain reaction, regardless of the genuine feelings of the individual.

The danger of this process is twofold: in the first place, the social pressure may prohibit the person from doing the type of mourning which will have a therapeutic result; secondly, the person by satisfying the social demands for a particular type of mourning (which is more often than not superficial) may substitute this surface mourning for the deep experience of mourning which is really necessary and thereby fail to find release. Erich Fromm has written of what he calls a socially patterned defect. By this he means that if an individual does not have genuine maturity, self-acceptance, spontaneity, he may be assumed to have a defect. When this defect is prevalent in a majority of the members of a society, it may be called a socially patterned defect. The significance of this defect in terms of my discussion is this: if the defect is so widespread, the person does not recognize it as a defect; since he is no different from the other members of his society, his security is not threatened.

What he may have lost in richness and in a genuine feeling of happiness is made up by the security he feels of fitting in with the rest of mankind —*as he knows them*. As a matter of fact, his very defect may have been raised to a virtue by his culture and thus give him an enhanced feeling of achievement. . . . Today we can meet a person who acts and feels like an automaton; we find that he never experiences anything which is really his; that he experiences himself entirely as the person he thinks he is supposed to be; that smiles have replaced laughter, meaningless chatter replaced communicative speech and *dulled despair has taken the place of genuine sadness* [italics mine].[11]

Real mourning and the therapeutic process which it entails are impossible for so many people because of the socially patterned defect which encourages man to shy away, not only from pain, but also from emotional involvement in life.

This survey of the contributions which have been made by various psychological studies of bereavement during the past half century indicates a trend of thought to which new insights and clinical data are being added. Grief is seen as a reaction which is far more complex than a mere sadness because of loss. It involves a severe disruption of the structure of the personality because of the loss which has been suffered. The deceased has left a void in one segment of the scheme in interpersonal relationships. Filling this void requires a new adjustment and integration of the personality of the bereaved.

[11] *Man for Himself* (New York: Rinehart & Co., Inc., 1947), pp. 221-23. Used by permission of the author.

Mourning is seen as a necessary part of this reintegration. Through the mourning process the bereaved has to go over and over memories which surrounded the deceased until he can be emancipated to assume new relationships within a framework from which the deceased has gone. This is a gradual and a painful process, but it must be confronted and undertaken honestly and courageously.

CHAPTER THREE

GRIEF AND THE MAN

W HEN WE APPROACH the funeral in its psychological dimension, we immediately become aware of the necessity for dealing with mourners as individuals. We concentrate on their feelings, their needs. The sensitive pastor will focus his attention on the dynamic forces which are underlying the behavior and attitudes of the mourners.

The Psychodynamics of the Grief Reaction

It is not my purpose to formulate a comprehensive catalogue of individual grief reactions. Rather I would suggest some of the major feelings which are characteristic of many bereaved individuals. We must guard against indiscriminate categorizing of mourners because these factors are extremely complex. They may be present in various individuals in widely different combinations. Therefore I do not present this material to set up departments into which types of mourners can be shunted but as a description of the many possible forces which may be active in the grief reaction of a particular individual.

These feelings do not necessarily have to be verbalized by the bereaved in order to be recognized. In fact, especially in the case of negative feelings, they may be pushed far from consciousness. The pastor will have to sharpen his awareness of the feelings of the individual, and properly reflect those feelings, if they are to play any part in the therapy of mourning. This is not to say that the pastoral counselor will probe for such feelings or that he will hasten to interpret feelings which the bereaved has not expressed.

So often in the past the major criterion for judging the success of the individual in coping with grief has been control of the emotions. The person who wept a great deal was viewed as one who was undergoing a severe reaction. The person who stoically accepted the situation was considered to have made an adjustment. Modern dynamic psychology gives us two fruitful and corrective insights at this point. In the first place, we must recognize individual differences in temperament and disposition. To expect the same degree of reaction in every individual is utterly unrealistic. In the second place, we must see that overreaction is not the only thing which should concern us. It is of utmost importance that underreaction, which is so often popularly interpreted as a successful adjustment, be recognized and given proper attention.

Tearfulness

One of the most common elements of the grief reaction is tearfulness. Grief, as has been indicated, is a painful experience which is often accompanied by periods of weeping. Thinking of or talking about the deceased appears to be the stimulus of the tearfulness. Such activities, summoning forth vivid memories of relationships which are now broken by death, are undoubtedly painful and are understandably accompanied by the normal reaction to pain— weeping.

On the other hand, there are sometimes reactions which are almost completely tearless, without any outward demonstration of emotional upset. The whole period following the death is faced with composure. In evaluating such a reaction one must ask: Is this behavior characteristic of the individual? Is this individual mourner typically a phlegmatic person? We know that there are some people who have been so conditioned in life that they exercise great control over their emotions. They do not easily become angered or upset; they never seem to be either extremely happy or very depressed. One would hardly expect such an individual to burst into floods of tears during bereavement.

However, such behavior may be uncharacteristic of the individual. When a normally responsive person reacts dully to bereavement, the awareness of the pastor must be sharpened to detect the dynamic forces which are responsible for the reaction which is not appropriate for this person. It is indicative that the person is not being himself because he hopes to delay or deny the painful grief reaction; because he bows to social convention; because his relationship with the deceased, consciously or unconsciously, gives rise to other feelings which are not compatible with the normally accepted reaction pattern.

An illustration of one of these motivations is Lindemann's comments on the grief reaction experienced by many of the burned and bereaved men after the Cocoanut Grove fire. Many of them were very tense physically as well as emotionally because of the stringency of their efforts to control themselves. They feared the possiblity of breaking down. This was not only because of their hesitancy to confront the pain of mourning, but also because of the value which our society attaches to the courage and control which are identified with masculinity. This is only one example of the way in which cultural pressures impinge upon the individual's right to express what he feels rather than what society decrees he ought to feel.

The fact that we recognize emotional and temperamental differences in people does not obviate a dynamic approach. Some individuals are phlegmatic and undemonstrative. Other persons are volatile, easily excited, with high pitches of emotional feeling. While we recognize these variations in people, we cannot be misled into oversimplification by this fact. The degree of feeling may vary according to the temperament of the individual, but we still must be aware of the need to examine and understand the dynamic forces which made the person what he is and which cause him to act as he does.

I have been speaking of tearfulness and composure as more or less external manifestations of feelings which lie beneath the surface. I turn now to some of the individual feelings which are often represented in grief situations.

Bewilderment and Loneliness

Bewilderment and loneliness are among the most common of such feelings. When someone who has been a part of our life's experience dies, some of the meaningfulness of life dies with him. The activities, feelings, and relationships of which his presence was a component part are deprived of meaning without him. Thus the whole pattern of life is upset. This confusion of the stuff of daily existence puts the mourner somewhat out of touch with reality. He is in a daze, apparently lost, even amid familiar surroundings. One focus of life has been lost, and until a new focus is found, the scheme of life is disorganized.

This chaotic experience adds to the difficulty of mourning. As I have said, mourning becomes therapeutic when the individual is capable of facing reality, assimilating the experience, and working out a new organization for living. Mrs. Nestor recently lost her husband. The situation was complicated by a quarrel with their youngest daughter, who left home after an argument with her father on the eve of his death, and who is still estranged from her mother. Mrs. Nestor now finds herself all alone in the farm home. She has disposed of all the farm animals which had filled her normal daily schedule with chores. She occupies herself with random activities about the house, making scrapbooks, puttering here and there. Her conversation is filled with remarks such as: "I just can't believe that Mr. Nestor is gone. Nothing seems right now. I'm so mixed up I can't think right. Some of the kids think I ought to come to live with them and sell the farm. I don't know what to do. I'm so mixed up I just can't trust my own judgment enough to make any decisions now." The confusion which has come to Mrs. Nestor's life as a result of the sudden breaking of two meaningful relationships is perfectly natural. Her life has to find a new orientation in reality before she will be released from these chaotic circumstances.

Closely related to these feelings of bewilderment is the feeling of loss. Death is a fearful enemy to men, not so much because they fear the end of their lives or the life of another, but because of the disturbing prospect of losing someone whom they need and love. Loneliness contributes heavily to the pain of the grief situation. William Rogers sums it up:

The death of a loved one is a painful experience, not because we fear what has happened or is happening to the loved one, but because of the loneliness that we ourselves are suffering. Our loved one is gone and there is only an aching void where once he was. The emptiness and change that have come to our lives are a bitter portion indeed. The experience is the more distressing because the ache is deep where no palliative can reach it.[1]

Grief places a tremendous stress upon the wholeness of the person. The deceased may have been very much a part of the life of the bereaved. Many instances could be cited of married couples who truly lived for each other, children who were devoted to their parents, mothers and fathers who made their children the focal point of their lives. When death breaks relationships such as these, there are bound to be both a terrible loneliness and a disruption of the whole concept of the self and its purpose in life. A loss such as this demands a new orientation of the self as the focus of a new and radically different field. Unless selfhood is maintained and strengthened, it will be very difficult for the individual to come through the painful experience of sorrow.

The therapy of mourning helps to relieve this feeling of terrible loss and loneliness. Facing the loneliness, talking about it, speaking of what the loss means to him, expressing the emptiness of life without the deceased, in some way help the mourner to be relieved. In the same manner sharing the feeling of loneliness with a friend or pastor helps to fill the vacuum which has been left by the loss. I have described in Chapter II the way in which such talking and social interaction are of therapeutic value. They offer a means of catharsis, an opportunity for the bereaved to examine and clarify his own feelings, and an occasion for the establishment of new relationships.

Fear

Another characteristic element of the grief reaction is fear. We may isolate several quite widely differing aspects of such fear. First would be the fear of death itself.

[1] From *Ye Shall Be Comforted,* in the Westminster Pastoral Aid Series, The Westminster Press, Philadelphia, Pa. Copyright 1950 by W. L. Jenkins. Used by permission.

The sophisticated modern mind is inclined to scoff at this fear as a vestigial superstition. Others would say that the fear of death is dispelled by a mature religious and philosophical viewpoint. But the fact remains, even for the man of faith, that in death finite man passes into infinity. It is the passing from the known into the unknown. Even those who heroically give their lives for a great humanitarian cause, sacrificing themselves for others, are subject to this fear.

The fear of death itself has nothing to do with the courage or bravery of a man. It is an ontological fear which has its roots in the very nature of man's being as a finite creature.

When one is confronted by the fact of the death of a loved one, this ontological fear is personalized. The fear of death is translated into individual terms. The passage into the infinite of one who has been known and loved, the recognition that death is the occasion for judgment, give rise to a natural trepidation regarding death.[2] While this pertains mostly to the death of the deceased, it is a natural transition for the mourner to think of his own demise as well. This is particularly true of mourners who are in the later years of life. Thus bereavement is often accompanied by the fear of death.

Another way in which fear is connected with death seems at first thought to be extremely remote, yet if we fully consider its psychological ramifications, we find that it is valid. It is entirely possible in some cases that the deceased is feared as well as mourned. In our sophisticated society we are beyond the superstitious belief in haunting spirits which must be placated with ritualistic observances. Any fear of the dead which would be found in modern man would be largely, if not completely, unconscious. But this does not make it any less real. In situations in which grief is accompanied by guilt there may be a concerted effort, unconsciously motivated, to placate the spirit of the deceased. This might take the form of idealization, effusive demonstrations of affection and honor, or lavish funerals. Such an attitude would make therapeutic work

[2] See Paul Tillich, *The Courage to Be* (New Haven: Yale University Press, 1952).

through mourning most difficult, if not impossible. The bereaved would form a morbid attachment to the deceased. Any breaking of the ties, which mourning requires, would only be the occasion for heightening the fear and in turn reinforcing it.

The most common form in which fear is related to death is the dread of the experiences which accompany death: the loneliness, the loss, the insecurity, the pain of mourning. We do not fear the end of our own lives so much as the suffering which we know our deaths will cause our loved ones. We do not fear the death of one of our family as much as the pain and suffering which we know will come to us and our fellow mourners. This is where fear and grief are most closely connected. The painful loss, the painful mourning, are the most dreaded consequences of death.

The tradition of the church shows a constant effort to encourage people in the face of death, that they feel no fear of it. Such endeavor is most certainly in harmony with the proclamation of the gospel. However, this at times may be an attack waged against a straw man, unless we broaden the concept of fear to include the other aspects which we have mentioned above, especially the fear of pain and suffering connected with death and mourning. Then, too, we realize that the way of dispelling this fear is not the frontal attack of exhortation and denial, that is, telling the person he has nothing to fear, but the way of recognition and understanding, that is, accepting the fearful feelings of the individual and aiding him to the achievement of understanding and perspective.

The feelings of bewilderment, loneliness, and fear are among the most common accompaniments of the grief reaction. Let us turn our consideration now to feelings which are not integral parts of every instance of bereavement, but which are very frequently seen in mourners. We should in no way minimize their importance because they are not a part of the common lot of all who mourn. In fact we should be more keenly aware of them and their dangerous results because of their lack of universality.

Ambivalence

Ambivalence, which can be described as simultaneous attraction and repulsion or simultaneous contradictory emotions, is a concept which gained major stature in the work of Freud. The possibility of both loving and hating a person is very real. When the object of this ambivalence has died, the complex situation becomes even more acute. "The loss of the love-object constitutes an excellent opportunity for the ambivalence in the love-relationship to make itself felt and come to the fore . . . to the effect that the mourner himself is to blame for the loss of the loved one, i.e., desired it." [3] Freud here makes two assertions: that ambivalent feelings are accentuated by the loss of the object of those feelings, and that ambivalence is a very real source for the feelings of guilt or hostility which often accompany bereavement. I shall explore this latter statement more fully when I discuss hostility and guilt in their relationship to grief.

Another phase of ambivalent feelings might arise in situations where there are both loss and gain connected with the death. While we cannot clearly isolate this as the contradiction between love and hostility, we can see a parallel tension involved. Robert G. was the son of a well-to-do merchant. The death of his father was a severe loss to the family, but it also meant that Robert inherited the family business. Virtually overnight his status was changed from that of a salaried employee to that of the owner and manager of the store. Both loss and gain were involved in the death of his father. This need not have been particularly damaging to the life of Robert. However, he had great difficulty in assimilating the grief experience, because a sense of guilt gnawed at him, putting into his mind the thought that perhaps he was really glad that his father had died because of the inheritance which he received. This was tantamount to disloyalty to his father and lack of filial devotion. His guilt feelings would not allow him to carry out effectively his new obligations nor find any satisfaction in his wealth.

Obviously this is not the case in every situation, but the pastor

[3] *Op. cit.*, p. 161.

Richmond Hill Library
2209 East Grace Street
Richmond, VA 23223

must constantly be aware of this possibility, asking the question: "How does this person see his loss and gain?" Unless this question is asked and answered, the ambivalent feelings may jeopardize the success of the work of mourning.

Hostility

Closely related to this discussion of ambivalence are feelings of hostility which sometimes come out in the reaction of grief. Hostile feelings may either blend in with feelings of affection and love or alternate with them. Just as in life interpersonal relationships are subject to varying degrees of harmony and conflict, feelings toward the deceased party of the relationship may take on different colorations.

Although there is a tendency to idealize the relationship with the deceased, perhaps the mourner also recalls certain hostilities which existed between them. For example, even when a husband and wife truly love each other, there are differences of opinion, likes and dislikes, annoying habits and variations in temperament. Both love and hostility are present in their relationship. When grief emerges, there is the possibility that it will be accompanied by hostile feelings. Mr. and Mrs. Abbott were a young couple who enjoyed a very happy marital relationship. After he returned from military service, Mr. Abbott put all his energy and financial resources into a struggling business which he had founded. In order to economize, he decided to allow his GI insurance to lapse. Mrs. Abbott was continually urging her husband to increase his insurance coverage, but he laughed off her concern, jokingly referring to her as a "golddigger." Then suddenly he died, leaving her without adequate economic undergirding. Creditors quickly took over the business, and Mrs. Abbott was forced to take a job shortly after the funeral. Although she deeply loved her husband and sincerely mourned his death, unconsciously she felt a burning resentment because of his improvidence. Her grief was motivated by her love for him, but there was also present a deep-seated hostility —a continuation of the ambivalence which existed in their relationship. It was impossible for her to achieve an adjustment in bereavement until the hostile feelings were recognized and dealt with.

Among the early psychoanalysts Freud, Groddeck and Alexander recognized that the grieving person is somehow an angry person and linked this anger and irritation with the frustration of any close human contact, a frustration and resentment which cannot be expressed because one does not get angry and mistreat one's mother or father, one's child or wife.[4]

This statement seems extreme if we think of hostility as a feeling directed against the deceased, for certainly not every instance of bereavement is accompanied by such feelings. However, if we accept hostility in the broader sense, as a symbolic representation of the outgrowth of the frustrations which are found in all of life, we can accept the universality of the phenomenon.

The bereaved person may recognize this hostility or may project it to others. Thus we often see grief-stricken parishioners, unwilling to recognize such hostility, becoming extremely antagonistic toward people who have been life-long friends or toward their pastor or family physician. They unreasonably blame these people for a great variety of difficulties, sometimes even attributing the cause of death to them. This may be the result of projecting onto others a hostility which is primarily directed against the deceased. The pastor will have to be very sensitive to the wide scope of such a situation, recognizing the hostility as a negative reaction which must be accepted and reflected if it is to become the occasion for growth. On the other hand, it may be a hostility which results from a desire to strike out against the situation which leaves the bereaved standing utterly helpless and frustrated. In either case it must be dealt with, for unless this is done, it will become an obstacle to the constructive and positive work of mourning.

Guilt

Feelings of hostility are almost inevitably complicated by feelings of guilt. We might explain this in terms of a tension between the

[4] Ina May Greer, "Grief Must Be Faced," *The Christian Century*, Feb. 28, 1945, p. 269.

feelings which were present in the relationship before death occurred and the feelings toward the deceased in the light of the fact that death has irrevocably broken the human relationship. Before death the relationship was one of ups and downs, love and resentment, agreements and disagreements. This was accepted as the normal pattern of human life, occurring even in the happiest of relationships. But in life there was opportunity to make up after disagreements, to prove love after expressing resentment, to look forward to victory after defeat. After death occurs, the same ambivalent feelings continue. But the opportunities for compromise, adjustment, and reconciliation are no longer present. Thus the mourner tends to idealize the deceased, thinking of him in the most glowing terms, emphasizing virtues, de-emphasizing faults. Then when the ambivalent feelings which have carried over from the previous relationship make themselves evident to the mourner, he feels terribly guilty—guilty because he sometimes feels hostile toward one whom he should always love, guilty because there is no way of atoning for these feelings, guilty because he did not appreciate the deceased while he had the chance. Similar reactions might be found in the death of an estranged member of the family. The bereaved may feel themselves responsible for causing the estrangement or for not effecting a reconciliation, and thus count themselves guilty.

The sorrowing person may blame himself for not giving the deceased proper care during a period of illness, for not perfectly fulfilling marital obligations, or for contributing in some way to the cause of death. The mourner reviews the entire relationship, scrutinizing his own actions and attitudes for things which he did wrong. He may find occasions when he was irritable, negligent, thoughtless, inconsiderate, unkind; or there may be some specific action upon which the guilt feeling hangs. Donald James, a college student, had serious difficulty dealing with his grief at the time of the death of his mother, not wishing to view her body in the casket or to enter her room at home, because he blamed himself for her death. He had been the driver of a car involved in an accident in which she had been injured. Although her death took place sometime later and was caused by something unrelated to her injuries in the accident, he felt that he was responsible. His guilt feelings made it difficult for him to meet and come through the grief experience. It makes no difference if these recriminations are based upon fact or imagination; they are a potent deterrent in the honest facing of grief.

There may be other cases of guilt feelings which have a basis in fact rather than imagination. Linda Lewis was the six-year-old daughter of a farm family. One day she was playing about the yard with her dog. The dog ran into a nearby pasture where two fractious cows were confined. Linda followed. After a while her parents missed her and began to hunt for the little girl. An hour later they found her in the pasture badly trampled by the cattle. Severely injured, she was rushed to a doctor and then the hospital. For two days she hung between life and death, finally dying in surgery. The pastor called in their home a number of times following Linda's death. Following are some excerpts from one of the conversations with Mrs. Lewis.

Mrs. Lewis: I still get mighty blue when I am all alone. I have to do some crying then.

Pastor: You still feel like crying some of the time.

Mrs. Lewis: I get to thinking about how it might have been. We knew those cows were bad. They have been mean all summer. That's why they were in the pasture by themselves. We have been meaning to ship them but just kept putting it off. How I wish we had gotten rid of them months ago!

Pastor: If you had sold the cattle, this might not have happened?

Mrs. Lewis: Yes, if only we hadn't kept putting it off, and for no good reason either.

Pastor: This makes you feel in a way responsible for what happened to Linda.

Mrs. Lewis: It's pretty hard to admit, but I guess we both think it.

Pastor: And it bothers you.

Mrs. Lewis: It's hard to give Linda up.

Pastor: And it's even tougher when you think that you were indirectly responsible for it.

Mrs. Lewis: Yes.

The deep sense of guilt, which both Mr. and Mrs. Lewis had, compounded the difficulty of their adjustment to the loss of their daughter.

There is another, and entirely different, way in which guilt feelings may arise. A person may feel very guilty because his actual feelings in the grief situation do not correspond with the way in which people of the community think he feels. Everyone may be praising him for his composure, the strength of his faith, the "wonderful way he is taking it," while inwardly he is torn by doubts, pain, and dejection. To him this situation is a source of guilt feelings. He feels guilty because he considers himself a hypocrite. Knowing that everyone is expecting him to be brave, he feels extremely guilty when he has moments which are not at all courageous. The experience of Rollin Moser illustrates this point. Mr. Moser was an elderly farmer who had recently lost his wife. The pastor called to ask him to take part in a laymen's service. This portion of their conversation shows the way in which guilt may be caused when actual feelings do not correspond with the way friends and neighbors think the bereaved feels.

Moser: As I told you over the phone the other night, I just can't accept that job you want me to do.

Pastor: You don't feel up to it?

Moser: It's not just that. Ever since the trouble a few months ago (*his wife's death*), people have been too good to me.

Pastor: They have done a lot for you.

Moser: They have done just everything for me. Everybody has been so good to me. That's the trouble—they've been too good (*tears in his eyes*).

Pastor: How do you mean they have been too good?

Moser: They have given me things and said such fine things. They have even written me letters. . . . Just a minute. . . . I want to show you something. (*He goes to a desk and gets a letter and a card written by two different people telling him how much they thought of his ability to overcome his grief and saying they were confident his great faith would carry him through.*)

Pastor: These are very sincere letters.

Moser: I know that. It's just because they are so sincere that it hurts me.

Pastor: You feel you are not worthy?

Moser: That's it exactly. I feel that I'm not able to live up to their expectations. They expect so much of me that I know I will not be able
to live up to it. I know they are sincere, and without meaning to do so
they are breaking my heart with kindness.[5]

The guilt which is felt under such circumstances prevents the individual from getting at his grief in its deepest aspects. It not only
confuses and confounds his feelings but also drives him further
away from the sense of reality which can alone provide the foundation for effectively working through grief.

Attention should also be called to the fact that guilt reactions,
especially those in which the mourner feels guilt because of some
real or imagined wrong done to the deceased, are often accompanied by actions which can be best understood as masochistic or
self-punishing. This really permeates a number of the reactions
which I have already described. An observer familiar with psychological data could easily see many examples of self-punishment in
various individual reactions. Some people in mourning draw into
an ascetic existence, punishing themselves by abnegation of the
pleasures of sociality. Others may punish themselves by plunging
into work, overactivity; literally burning themselves up under the
guise of keeping busy. Masochism is also detected in efforts on the
part of the mourner designed to perpetuate the memory of the
deceased in a morbid, nontherapeutic way. In some communities
all the clocks in the house of mourning are set at the hour when
the person died. Sometimes pictures are taken of the corpse in the
coffin. More common reactions of this type include keeping all
the belongings of the deceased intact, keeping the house "just like it
was when Mother died," setting an extra place at the table. Although these may be the more bizarre examples of such a self-
punishing reaction, there are other less extreme instances which
follow the same general pattern to which the pastor must be sensitive.

Masochism is recognized psychologically as an outlet for ag-
gressions. Since the person feels unable to vent his hostile and

[5] Rollin A. Johnson, "Rollin Moser," unpublished case study, Federated Theological
Faculty, University of Chicago, 1950.

aggressive feelings against others, he turns them upon himself. This is what Rosenzweig called "nemesism." The guilt and hostile feelings which often accompany grief, coupled with the frustration of a loss about which the person can do nothing, are turned inward upon the self.

Idealization

Another distinctive characteristic of the grief reaction is found in the tendency for the mourner to idealize the deceased. I have already spoken of the part which remembering the deceased plays in the mourning process. Lindemann and Rogers make a good deal of the importance of being able to remember and to live with the memory of the deceased. This remembering activity is often highly colored by accentuating the virtues and positive values of the deceased. There are a number of possible motives which might underlie this reaction. Sometimes this idealization is a by-product of appreciation. The mourner expresses his appreciation for what the deceased did or meant to him by enhancing his character and virtues. Or the enhancement may be the result of the cultural taboo against speaking ill of the dead. Or it may be due to an effort to compensate for obvious and known faults in the deceased. These deficiencies are seen as a threat to the reputation of the deceased. Since he can do nothing now to amend his character or reputation, the mourner assumes a responsibility to minimize the flaws and to accentuate the virtues. Or it is possible to see a connection between idealization and guilt feelings in the bereaved. Praising the deceased seems to be one way in which guilt feelings can apparently be relieved. However, this can be only a temporary relief, because as the character of the deceased is enhanced and he becomes a more worthy object of love, the mourner is all the more blameworthy for his neglect or failure to appreciate.

In a sense the fact that religion sees a judgmental aspect in death also contributes to the motivation for idealization. This does not mean that death is to be viewed as judgment in the sense of punishment. But Christianity views death as the end of man's pilgrimage upon earth, the point at which his striving to work out his own salvation with fear and trembling comes to an end. Recognizing this, in all probability unconsciously, the mourner may naïvely attempt to contribute to his loved one's spiritual well-being by accentuating his positive values and minimizing his flaws.

The Effect of Personality Structure

Before this chapter on the description of various aspects of the grief reaction is closed, one further dimension should be explored. In a way I have fragmentized the experience of bereavement and the reaction to it. In order to approach the subject from a different angle, I turn to an analysis offered by Karen Horney.[6] Through this device I hope to show that the content of the grief reaction is somewhat determined by the type of person who mourns.

Although we would not attempt to follow out all the ramifications of the typologies set up by Doctor Horney and their applications to neuroses, we can see some correlation between the variations of the grief experience and the basic types of individuals she describes. She speaks of individuals who may be characterized as moving toward people, moving against people, and moving away from people. We need not restrict this typology to the neurotics, although the pattern would seem to be more firmly set in such cases. The basic typologies are applicable to the "normal" individual when we see them blended, with one or another type of attitude and behavior dominant.

The individual who moves toward people views himself as a more or less helpless person. He requires the support and assistance of others in making his way through life. The relationships which he forms in all probability will be relationships of dependence. He strives to attach himself to the strong. When such a person is confronted by loss, it is easily seen that a severe disorientation will result. He has lost not only an object of affection, but also a source of strength. The severity of his loss will be mirrored in his grief reaction, and his adjustment to the experience of bereavement will be determined by his characteristic moving toward people. We

[6] *Our Inner Conflicts* (New York: W. W. Norton & Co., 1945).

might see such a person waging a determined campaign to seek sympathy and comfort. He needs someone to lean upon. There is the possibility that mourning will be ineffective for him because it is his intention to gain support rather than to adjust to his loss. Because he is inclined to rate himself by what others think of him, he may easily fall into conventional patterns of mourning in order to gain their sympathy without any regard for the lack of help which these patterns provide for him. Because of his extreme attachment to the deceased, genuine mourning is requisite for any adjustment. Yet if great care is not taken, his basic dependency and need for a center of power outside himself will preclude any possibility of therapeutic mourning.

The individuals who move against people are described as those who are the fighters, the hostile, the rebellious. They regard with suspicion the feelings and intentions of the people who surround them. Not only are they on guard against others, but they strike out against them. Loss for them can also be very real. However, it is not the loss of someone to whom they were attached, but rather the loss of someone whom they exploited, from whom they gained. Their lack of capacity for love does not prevent them from experiencing bereavement. Mourning is extremely difficult for this type of individual. He despises any indication of weakness and interprets all emotions or feelings as sentimentality. The emotional experience which is involved in grief must be denied and pushed far away because to give in to it would be the admission of weakness. It could also be supposed that the hostile, exploitative relationships which are sustained by such an individual could be the source of very real guilt feelings in a situation of loss. This would further complicate the work of mourning.

The third category, those who move away from people, desire neither to belong nor to fight. They live in a sense of isolation from their fellow men, existing in a world of their own devising. They are isolated, not in the sense that they do not sustain relationships with others, but in that they do so without spontaneity. They are capable of loving, but they do not particularly want to love. Loss would not be as serious for them as for the other types of individuals I have described. The attachments which they form in life are not particularly filled with feeling and meaning, either positive or negative. In a way mourning does not pose too much of a problem for such a detached individual. And yet it does. This type of person hates to conform to established patterns of conduct, but in order to avoid friction, he will do so. He would look upon mourning as something which is completely unnecessary. He would prefer to intellectualize what we commonly call emotion. Yet in order to avoid setting himself against the social group, he would conform with any established patterns, no matter what he actually felt. Mourning, then, is a problem for him, not because he cannot adjust to the loss of the deceased, but because mourning is a practice which he endures under community pressure in spite of the toll which it exacts from his freedom to express himself.

We must grant that these types have been presented in most extreme and generalized fashion. In actuality we would probably find them working in combination within individuals with whom we deal. Yet it is not wrong to presume that variations of the dominant tendencies which we have described can be seen functioning in this fashion in particular individuals. This material also forces us to recognize not only that the problems and difficulties which people confront in bereavement are due to the situation in which they find themselves, but that the personality structure of the individual is a significant factor in the success or failure of his mourning.

As the pastor works with bereaved parishioners, as he visits them before and after the funeral, as he prepares to conduct the funeral services, he will have to evaluate in his own mind the needs of the individual. He will have to be familiar with the psychological information which is available to assist him in understanding the feelings and the needs of the mourner. He will have to ask himself the question: "What are legitimate needs, and what needs require transformation?" His answer to this question will be conditioned by asking a further query: "How is my interpretation of the parishioner's needs different from the way he feels his needs?" These questions must be faced and answered honestly and intelligently if the funeral service is to be a beneficial and therapeutic experience rather than an empty ceremony.

CHAPTER FOUR

THE FUNCTION OF THE FUNERAL

THE ESTABLISHMENT of evaluative criteria regarding funeral services and practices is not an easy task. The subject is complex because it must be approached in several dimensions. The funeral is a religious observance of the Christian Church. Therefore it has theological foundations and implications. The funeral is also a social observance, an event which involves a community of individuals. As such it possesses a relationship to the culture which both derives from the culture and contributes to it. And I have undertaken to investigate a psychological or personal dimension of the funeral which deals with the value and meaning of the funeral for the individual and his needs.

I would be guilty of a grievous error if I presumed to suggest that the funeral services and practices could be fully understood through any one of these three dimensions. Each aspect—the theological, the cultural, and the psychological—makes a distinctive and unique contribution which in turn interacts with the contributions of the other aspects. We cannot say that we should be concerned only with the theological implications of the funeral and let the rest go by the board any more than we can say that the only important thing about a funeral is the psychological aspect, to the utter disregard of the theological and cultural. We must see these three dimensions impinging upon one another, interacting, enriching, complementing.

Although the major thrust of the material which I have presented is psychologically oriented, it is not to be assumed that psychology is being used to displace either the theological or the cultural understanding of the funeral. It is my purpose to add psychologically relevant data to the body of knowledge which has already been developed around the theological and social understanding of funeral practices. However, this task must be undertaken *within* a theological and cultural framework. Therefore in developing evaluative criteria we must take into consideration all the dimensions of the subject which we investigate.

The Purpose of the Funeral

What is the purpose of the funeral? This question can be answered in a number of ways. Andrew Blackwood says:

> What are the reasons for holding a funeral service? The chief aim is to glorify God. The best way to do that in the presence of death is to administer comfort. As the root idea of the word makes clear, to comfort means to strengthen in the Lord. Both in making the arrangements and in carrying them out, the pastor strives to bring the people into right relations with God, so that they will accept his plan for their altered lives.[1]

This might be called a theocentric purpose, designed to undergird a belief in the sovereignty of God in death and life. Man's comfort is seen as the faith that even though God has brought to pass an alteration in life, he will provide the strength which is needed to assimilate the experience of loss. However, Blackwood is speaking out of his Presbyterian heritage of Calvinism in this definition. His statement would be subject to reinterpretation if the theological coloration were changed. But virtually all Protestant definitions of the purpose of the funeral would include the theocentric in the sense of making available to the mourning individuals the comforting knowledge of God's love, with or without the predestinarian overtones of Calvinistic theology. We can say, then, that one of the purposes of the funeral is to relate people to God in such a way that they can draw upon the resources of God's spirit in their hour of confusion and need.

Another purpose of the funeral which is losing acceptance in most of Protestantism in our time is a corollary of the theocentric purpose: a hortatory purpose. In the past many funerals provided an opportunity to sound a word of warning to the mourners that

[1] From *The Funeral,* copyright 1942 by The Westminster Press. Used by permission.

they mend their sinful ways and prepare for their own death. Use of the funeral for exhortation and/or evangelism is no longer practiced in the main streams of Protestantism, putting an end to an approach which very often took unfair advantage of the mourner. The damaging effects of such funerals in heightening guilt feelings and breeding hostility reduced the possibility for the church to aid people to mourn. Instead of drawing individuals closer to the church and the resources for comfort which it possesses, it served to alienate them and compound their grief.

A third purpose of the funeral includes the aspect of fellowship, the community of the Christian Church. Ideally in the beloved community the joys of one are the joys of all and the sorrows of one the sorrows of all. In this we can see another very real purpose for the funeral. It allows the beloved community to express its concern at the loss of one of its number. The religious significance of this fellowship must be brought out, because only within the Christian framework will there be the opportunity for the unique blend of mutuality and individuality which keeps this fellowship from becoming an oppressive agent of social pressure and convention. In other words, if the beloved community fulfills its true function, it will share the grief of the bereaved but will not enforce a pattern of mourning which is incompatible with the feelings of the mourner.

Finally, the funeral has a psychological function to establish a climate for therapeutic mourning. Since this is the subject with which I am dealing in detail, I shall not explicate it fully here. But I would say that this fourth purpose operates in harmony with the first and third purposes which I have proposed. They are not to be looked upon as contradictory or mutually exclusive. They work in harmony toward the end that those who mourn shall be comforted.

The purposes of the funeral which have been outlined here stem directly from the sources of the funeral. Religious services and burial rituals at the time of death are not without reason or meaning. They meet a very deep human need. It would be possible to say that if we did not have provision for them in the Christian tradition, we would have to invent them.

Let us trace the sources of funeral ritual and practices in the three dimensions which have been set up: the theological, the cultural or social, and the individual or psychological.

Theological Sources of the Funeral

In a study of the theological origins for funeral ritual and practice we are confronted with a number of Christian interpretations of death and its meaning. It is not my intention to describe them in detail but only as they are related to the funeral.

The Scripture has surprisingly little to say of death. Nowhere is its place in the economy of nature discussed. Death is seen as a mystery, a stark reality which every man must face, but nevertheless inexplicable. Death is viewed as a state or condition, representing a belief in some kind of existence beyond the grave. The teachings of Jesus contain no explanation of death as a physical phenomenon, although they demonstrate a deep understanding of the loss which is sustained by the mourners through death. Jesus laid no emphasis upon death as an evil in itself. The Pauline epistles offer an interpretation of death as the wages of sin which can be seen in two ways. Either it rests upon a rabbinical interpretation of death in terms of the fall of man, which finds no support in the gospel, or it refers to spiritual rather than physical death. Obviously the latter contains a great deal of truth. Reinhold Niebuhr says:

While there is a profound difference between attributing sin to mortality and deriving mortality from sin, the Pauline interpretation of death nevertheless lends itself to dualistic interpretations. It is not at all clear that St. Paul consistently regards physical death as the consequence of sin. At any rate he frequently uses the concept of death symbolically to designate spiritual death, as for instance when he speaks of the man who is "dead in trespasses and sins" (Eph. 2:1). Furthermore his classical assertion that the "sting of death is sin" (I Cor. 15:56) can hardly be interpreted to mean that mortality as such is the consequence of sin. On the contrary, it seems in complete accord with the general Biblical view of the relation of sin to mortality. In this view mortality, insecurity and dependence are not of themselves evil but become the occasion of evil when man seeks in his pride to hide his mortality, to overcome his insecurity by his own power and to establish his independence.[2]

Obviously this matter is far more complex than this discussion indicates explicitly. I have simplified the issue considerably with the intention of showing only the bold outline of the New Testament view of human mortality.

Based upon the understanding of spiritual references to death, there are three basic theological interpretations of the meaning of death which have a bearing upon the justification for funeral rituals. All of these three are permeated with a sense of the mystery of death. First, there is the view that death is punishment for sin. As I have said, there is very little scriptural basis for this position because there seems to be good reason to interpret any such references to death as speaking of spiritual rather than natural or physical death. Yet we can see the impact of the interpretation of death as punishment in funeral ritual. This is the basis for the judgmental and hortatory emphases of some funeral services. The reading of passages from the Bible such as "Remove thy stroke away from me: I am consumed by the blow of thine hand" (Ps. 39:10), or, "For we are consumed by thine anger, and by thy wrath are we troubled" (Ps. 90:7), can be easily understood by the mourner as an indication that death is a punishment from God. Sermons which are used as a device to scold the family for spiritual laxity, and so on, can be interpreted the same way. Therefore one of the theological justifications for the funeral is that it provides an opportunity to present the judgment of God in death and an appeal for repentance.

A second, and far more prevalent, theological understanding of death carries the idea that death is the will of God. We see it in the early Church. J. T. McNeill speaks of a letter of consolation which was written by Jerome:

In health or sickness he rejoices in God's will. We are not born to live forever here. We should mourn only for those of the dead who are in

[2] *The Nature and Destiny of Man* (New York: Charles Scribner's Sons, 1941), I, 173-74. Used by permission of the publisher.

Gehenna, but rejoice that Blaesilla has passed to the realm of light. He seeks to dissuade Paula from fasting and mourning for her daughter: mourning is for those who wear silk, not for the religious. He goes to some pains to interpret Scripture passages on mourning as offering no pattern to be imitated by the bereaved Christian, and presents the example of a Christian lady bereaved of her husband and sons, who smilingly vowed herself to fuller service to Christ than before.[3]

Confronted with the mystery of death, man feels very inadequate in himself. The only way of bringing any logic to bear upon his loss is to see it as a part of the responsibility of some power greater than his. Man must view death seriously. He has no choice but to accept it. Hence he sees it not as accidental, but as purposeful; and the purpose is God's. The funeral in the light of this interpretation of death becomes an occasion for understanding and accepting the will of God in life and death. It has a supportive function because it also presents the availability of God as a source of strength. As we see God's will in the coming of death, we can also rely upon his will to help us through the troublous times of bereavement.

The third theological understanding of death sees it as a natural part of life. Physical man is mortal; death is a part of the normal human experience. In the sense that God is the creator, the founder of the natural law, God is the initiator of death; but death comes as the result of a physical condition or accidental coincidence. With such an understanding of death the funeral is an occasion for comprehending both the nature of man and the nature of God. Man's mortality is frankly recognized and accepted, as is man's inability to deal with the crisis. God's love and providence are seen as the aid which man needs as he confronts the mystery of death and the pain of his own loss. The funeral, then, is a way of presenting the need and the means for adjusting to the loss which has been sustained through death. It is to provide comfort in the fullest sense of the word.

Christian theology is not concerned with death alone, but also with resurrection. While it is virtually impossible to explore fully

[3] *Op. Cit.*, p. 103. Used by permission of Harper & Bros.

within the scope of this discussion the meaning of the Christian doctrine of the resurrection, we must recognize that the fact of the resurrection has an important bearing upon the source and motivation of funeral ritual. Without getting involved in various interpretations of the resurrection, I can say that its primary emphasis is that death for the Christian is not the end, but that new life is possible after death.

St. Paul was convinced that "flesh and blood cannot inherit the kingdom of God; neither doth corruption inherit incorruption" (I Cor. 15:50). But this conviction did not drive him to the conclusion that everlasting life annuls all historical reality for which "the body" is the symbol. He believed rather that "it is sown a natural body and is raised a spiritual body" and that the consummation means not to "be unclothed, but clothed upon" (II Cor. 5:4). In that succinct phrase the Biblical hope of a consummation which will sublimate rather than annul the whole historical process is perfectly expressed. It is not possible to give a fuller or more plausible account of what is implied in the Christian hope of the fulfillment of life; and it is well to remember that the conditions of finiteness make a more explicit definition of the consummation impossible. It is therefore important to maintain a decent measure of restraint in expressing the Christian hope. Faith must admit "that it doth not yet appear what we shall be." But it is equally important not to confuse such restraint with uncertainty about the validity of the hope that "when he shall appear, we shall be like him; for we shall see him as he is" (I John 3:2).[4]

The Christian's experience of death, then, is viewed as a transition or translation from one life to another. Rogers puts it this way:

The loved one is not gone, but gone before, and in a later life we shall meet him, and know him, and have fellowship with him again. Death of our loved one may be all loss for us at the time, but it is all gain for our beloved, and in the long run of eternity it will be all gain for us too. And acceptance of this doctrine helps us to evaluate our grief correctly. We see clearly now that our pain is for our own loneliness, and that it is on this basis that we shall have to work it out. This is not to minimize our pain, but it is to understand it. This doesn't take our pain away, but it does aid in formulating a plan for overcoming it.[5]

[4] Niebuhr, op. cit., II, 298. Used by permission of the publisher.
[5] Op. cit., p. 43.

The Christian funeral is a witness to the hope of the resurrection and the possibility of continued interaction with the deceased, for the historical is not annulled but changed in the resurrection.

Cultural Sources of the Funeral

In addition to these theological origins or justifications of the funeral, we can isolate some cultural sources of funeral practices. In many primitive cultures we can see burial rites which were designed to appease the spirit of the deceased or to prevent him from returning to do harm to the living. So steps were taken to prevent or obviate his spirit's return. The body was either destroyed by fire or some other means which would make for speedy disintegration or was confined beneath large heaps of rocks. The possessions of the deceased, sometimes even members of his family, were destroyed with him in order to remove any reason his spirit might have for returning. All these rites were basically self-protective.

Sometimes funeral services are intended as a dramatization of the loss which has been experienced by the family and friends of the deceased. The mourning of biblical times might be said to come in this category. There is no reference to any religious observance connected with the burial, but there was a definite ceremony of mourning by family and friends and by professional mourners, who in their wailing and chanting would recite the good qualities of the deceased and the extent of the loss which the family was called upon to bear.[6] In a sense the modern funeral can be understood in the same way, as a manifestation of the loss which is felt by the bereaved.

The cultural taboos regarding death also influence the development of funeral practices. In our time death has been regarded as a taboo subject, and oftentimes our funerals reflect this taboo. We do not like to think or talk about death, preferring either to push its reality completely from our minds or to cover it with a variety of disguises. We are repelled on the one hand by the frightening mystery which surrounds death and our helplessness in the face of it, and on the other hand by the pain of the loss which accompanies

[6] See "Mourning" in Hastings' *Dictionary of the Bible.*

it. In keeping with the optimistic overtones of our culture, we attempt to escape from frustration and unpleasantness in life; and we carry this attempt into the experience of bereavement. George Buttrick has presented this fact in striking fashion:

The evasion is carried into daily practice, as we might expect. When a man is critically sick, the doctor does not tell him. His friends are likely to assure him, "You look much better today." The minister is advised that it might be wiser if he did not see him: "He might think he is going to die." If the minister asks, "Well, isn't he, sometime?" the family circulates the word that the church should have a happier-spirited minister. Meanwhile the man's wife searches for insurance policies and the will, and perhaps finds neither; he has written none, because he might think he is going to die. When he does die, the undertaker strives to make it appear that he has not died; he dresses him in a tuxedo, and lays him in a narrow box as if he were asleep, even though a man does not usually sleep in a tuxedo in a narrow box. There is a funeral, for, unfortunately for our evasions, the man *has* died: "Too bad about So-and-so. But let's not think about it!" So we run to our familiar hiding place in the sensate world. And the cynic calls religion an "escape!" In truth, religion alone refuses to be blind to the fact of death.[7]

The denial of the reality of death in our culture is closely associated with the tremendous value which our generation places upon youth, vitality, and activity. There is a great and unconscious fear of growing old. Although medical science is making it possible to live long, we do not regard this as a benefit unless it is also possible to retain the physical characteristics and energies of youth. We commonly think of the aging process as bad. Biologically aging is dying, with the human body ceasing its growth and beginning devolution at about the twentieth year. Then the struggle begins, women striving to retain the bloom of youth's beauty and men striving to maintain virile energy and productiveness. This whole cultural pattern reinforces the fear of death because it is the negation of the life we prize.

[7] *Christ and Man's Dilemma*, pp. 85-86. Copyright 1946 by Stone & Pierce. Used by permission of Abingdon-Cokesbury Press.

Earl Loomis, a Pennsylvania psychiatrist, has suggested:

The reason the mortician, not the pastor, is often called by a family is because he symbolizes "unctuousness." He is thought of as a salve-applier, as a master of denial. Death is sacred, or lovely, or unreal; he is associated with soft music or the perfume of flowers. People grasp for denial first, and the mortician symbolizes it.[8]

While this is a very subtle distinction, it does indicate one of the ways in which the cultural pattern of denying the reality of death has an effect on the funeral.

This pattern is also related to burial practices. The denial of the reality of death is mirrored in efforts to preserve the body for a long period of time. Caskets and vaults capitalize upon the fact that their use will prevent deterioration of the body for many years, almost as if to suggest that the actual end of the person's physical existence could be postponed indefinitely. In a very oblique sense the mourners are led to feel that they are able to retain possession of their loved one for many years. This is in essence a denial of the reality and the finality of the experience of death.

When we speak of cultural origins, we must remember that most cultural patterns were established with a very definite reason and purpose behind them. They can hardly be called accidents because they fill a human need. But as time passes, the rationale of a custom is lost. People observe the pattern only out of force of habit. The custom becomes outmoded because it no longer fulfills the purpose for which it was begun. We can see this in some of the customs connected with bereavement.

For example, the culture has provided a means by which a person can mourn, a way of reducing the pain and tension of grief. Customarily a period has been set apart for mourning, when the bereaved can depart from normal behavior, receive special attention from friends and relatives, be freed from the regular obligations of life, be set apart as an individual whose feelings should not be intruded upon. Society will respect his desire to avoid many social

[8] From "Funerals in the Light of Our Knowledge of Grief and Bereavement," Summarized Report of Joint Session of May 5, 1950, Department of Pastoral Services, Commission on Religion and Health, Federal Council of Churches.

contacts or to be preoccupied with his thoughts of the deceased for a few days. Such customs were a very good thing in their original intention. They provided for a climate in which the therapy of mourning could work. But then the patterns became outmoded. People no longer knew why they were doing certain things during bereavement. They only did them because everyone else did. The customs thus lost much of their meaning and most of their value.

An illustration of this might be seen in the custom of wearing special mourning garb. The wearing of a traditional black garb was originally intended to set the mourner apart, to insure that he would have the opportunity to do the work of mourning without intrusion from other people or responsibilities. The custom of wearing mourning clothes has been modified somewhat, but dark clothing is still considered proper for mourning. Most people, when death occurs in their family, purchase new clothing to wear at the funeral. But the fact that mourning garb is no longer worn after the funeral by many people indicates that it is not serving any purpose other than compliance with particular funeral customs. In fact, quite often there is a rebellion against the somber garb immediately after the funeral, and people sometimes revert to brighter than usual clothing.

Or we could see the same phenomenon occuring in the matter of burial. Originally the body was buried to allow it to deteriorate. This custom was helpful because it demonstrated very dramatically that the person was really dead, that the physical relationships which had been enjoyed with that person were now at an end. This sense of finality provided a strong impetus for the reorganization of life without the presence of the deceased. We still bury the dead, but our sensibilities and our desire to evade the reality of death make preservation and not deterioration the major goal. Improved embalming methods and special vaults make burial possible without rapid deterioration. Therefore even after burial there is still a subtle sense of physical presence and reality.

Still another evidence of outmoded custom is seen in a recent development of a cemetery visiting service on the West Coast. Originally the custom of visiting the grave of the deceased may have had therapeutic value in recalling memories of the deceased and in emphasizing the finality of death and burial. Families of the deceased would make periodic visits to the grave. But now, indicating the way in which the empty form of a custom can be continued without any of its original content, a cemetery visiting service will assume this function for the mourner. Its advertisement states:

Do you have loved ones reposing somewhere in the ———— metropolitan area and are unable to visit? I will personally attend any cemetery, mausoleum, memorial park, crematorium or columbarium; offer respects in your behalf and mail confirmation of visit. Give name of cemetery and deceased. Give identity number of grave or niche. Visiting fee $3 minimum. Flowers put on grave or niche for $2 additional plus cost of flowers ($5 minimum). Photograph taken of grave and mailed you for $5 extra.

The church has very often attacked the cultural patterns which surround the funeral. Usually this has been a justifiable opposition to meaningless and valueless customs. However, if we can see some value in the original intention of many of these practices, it may be that the proper function of the church is either to revive the true meaning of the pattern consistent with the Christian interpretation of the meaning of death and mourning, or to invent new patterns which are relevant to the actual situation, not the situation which some disinterested person theorizes into existence.

Psychological Sources of the Funeral

This brings us to the third category of origins, the psychological. As was said at the beginning of this chapter, it is impossible to separate these three categories because they are not mutually exclusive. They are blended together in human existence. The psychological interacts with both the theological and the cultural sources because the central focus of all three is human need. Thus much of what can be said of the psychological origins is only a summary of what has already been stated above.

The funeral is important psychologically as an occasion which dramatizes the need for mourning. It is designed as a meaningful event in the life of the mourner which publicly recognizes his loss and which offers the opportunity for that loss to be shared by the community. This sharing is important to the bereaved not only because of the mutuality of the experience but also because it symbolizes the acceptance of his feelings.

The psychological consequence of the Christian funeral is also seen in the provision of divine and human love for the bereaved without demanding love in return. The traumatic experience of loss in many instances deprives the mourner of the capacity to love. Thus any expression of sympathy, concern, and support which does not demand reciprocity is of benefit to him. The funeral provides such an experience.

The funeral is also based upon a psychological need for the individual to feel the meaning of death. This means that he must interpret death in his own experience before he is able to understand it on an intellectual or theological level. He must be freed from the deceased through mourning before it is possible for him to comprehend the theological interpretation of death in a way which will be meaningful for him. Thus the funeral is intended to aid him in realizing and understanding what has happened in his own experience.

As the last of the psychological justifications for the funeral, I would propose that it sounds a note of finality which is in keeping with both Christian doctrine and the psychological understanding of mourning. It seems that the funeral is in part an instinctive accompaniment to the note of finality which death brings. The service lends a dignity and meaning to the culmination of life. As John Wesley exclaimed in his *Journal,*

Oh what a difference is there between the English and the Scotch method of burial! The English does honour to human nature, and even to the poor remains, that were once a temple of the Holy Ghost! But when I see in Scotland a coffin put into the earth, and covered up without a word spoken it reminds me of what was spoken concerning Jehoiakim, "He shall be buried with the burial of an ass." [9]

[9] May 20, 1774.

A life's record is being closed, and there is an instinctive call on the part of the mourners to see that life's record is finished properly and fittingly. The bereaved will not achieve the therapeutic effect of mourning so long as he has a sense of unfinished business hanging over him. The funeral, coming as the climax to the experiences which immediately follow death, is designed to bring to a focus these experiences and feelings. It does not mean that the mourning process is over, but that the physical relationship with the deceased is now at an end.

This treatment of the various sources of funeral ritual and practices and the justification for them is admittedly descriptive. As I turn to the task of establishing criteria for evaluating contemporary funerals, I shall have to become more critical.

Criteria for Evaluating the Personal Function of the Funeral

The sources and justifications of the funeral are considered under three major categories: the theological, the cultural, and the psychological. I shall employ these same categories with some minor rearrangement in my proposal of evaluative criteria. The theological category will remain the same. However, what I have said of the cultural aspect of the problem, that is, that cultural patterns were originally designed to be helpful in meeting human needs, and that as time passes, they lose their meaning and become compulsive rituals, indicates that some of the material which was discussed as a cultural source of the funeral will now be considered in the category which I label psychological. The residue, for the purpose of establishing criteria, will be the substance of a new category, the aesthetic.

Because the funeral is a religious service, it must be conducted within a theological framework. We cannot see it as a psychological device in a purely secular context. Thus in order to work with the funeral service in an effort to improve its personal function, we must see it as a whole. The theological, aesthetic, and psychological criteria must be compatible rather than competitive. None of the three categories can be set up as inviolable, to which the

others must concede and bow. They are interrelated on a very deep
level by their concern for the welfare of man, the basic integrity
which they make possible in the self.

Every funeral service has an implicit or explicit theological position. Our task is to determine what that position is and the degree
to which it is helpful in enabling man to relate the deep truths of
our Christian faith to his needs.

One question which must be asked is: Does the funeral deal
realistically with death? Christianity properly prides itself upon
being realistic and successfully resisting many attempts through the
centuries which would make it an avenue of escape from the stern
realities of life. The traditional Christian faith has never permitted
a retreat from the fact of death. It has recognized the ever-nearness
of death as part of the existential situation in which man lives.
This is one of the realities which a thinking Christian must face.
In like fashion death has been viewed seriously because it is one
of the crises of life. It involves not only a radical departure from
the past, a breaking of a pattern of living and all the relationships
and activities which are entailed. It also involves for the Christian
the beginning of a new life. The Christian doctrine of the resurrection witnesses to belief that death is real, but that it is not the
end of existence. It is a transition to a new quality of life. Death
breaks the pattern of human relationships; resurrection holds out
the possibility that a new quality of relationships can be established
in a later life.

The Christian doctrines of death and resurrection provide a very
valuable tool for understanding grief. The mourner sorrows because of the pain of his loneliness and confusion, not because
of the fact that death has come. This does not say that there is no
pain for the Christian mourner, but it does enable him to see his
feelings in the proper perspective. However, if the reality of death
is denied, the value of the doctrine of the resurrection is negligible.

The doctrine of the resurrection is a Christian concept which
must be distinguished from the Greek idea of immortality. Resurrection includes two major themes: (1) the Christian by virtue
of his acceptance of the grace of God through faith receives the

gift of eternal life, a rebirth, a new quality of life in the here and now; (2) eternal life reaches its full fruition after death occurs, when the Christian enters a new dimension of life. On the other hand, immortality presents the thesis that there is in man an immortal entity which continues its existence uninterrupted after its separation from the body by death. The philosophical concept of immortality is quite different from the doctrine of the resurrection in that immortality is presented as something which is inherent in the being of man. This is both an evasion of the reality of death and a subtle form of human pride. Resurrection is a presentation of the inexhaustible goodness and power of God rather than of man. The same resources of God which make the resurrection possible are available to assist the bereaved in his difficult work of mourning.

Since the funeral is recognized as a religious rite, a portion of its attention is turned toward God. Its purpose is to present a vision of God which will be of comfort and help to the mourners in their suffering. It would seem that there are two main currents in the way in which the spirit of God is presented to bereaved individuals. On the one hand, there is an emphasis upon the sovereignty of God. The power of God over human life is emphasized. God is pictured as the giver of life and the one who takes life away. Death then is seen as a direct result of the will of God. In a very extreme sense this view makes of the funeral an occasion for glorifying God, who has brought this painful experience to the mourner. It can easily develop into either asceticism or fatalism. The over-all effect of such a view would seem to build up a barrier between God and man at a time when man needs to feel the nearness of God and God's concern for his plight. It presents a vision of God which is not too helpful in stimulating the therapeutic work of mourning. A view of the sovereignty of God which allows no freedom, which is not conditioned by the gift of a free will for man, permits very little growth for man. It fosters a spirit of irresponsibility. Applied to the subject of mourning, it would encourage the bereaved to sit back and wait for God to comfort him,

without interpreting mourning as a process in which the spirit
of God works within man to restore health and bring about growth.

This view is sometimes modified by speaking of a divine purpose
which is embodied in the universe. Death, then, is shown *sub
specie aeternitatis* as a part of the carrying out of this universal
purpose. If this is interpreted narrowly, it can have the same effect
as the insistence upon the utter sovereignty of God described above.
If, however, it is given a wider interpretation, including therapy
and growth as part of the divine purpose, its results can be much
more beneficial. One might put it in these terms: If the description
of the divine purpose of God for the universe, which is made at a
time when the stark reality of death is being confronted, includes
a vital emphasis upon the creative aspects of that purpose, the relationship between God and man will be strengthened rather than
weakened.

The other main current in the way in which the spirit of God
is presented to the bereaved places the emphasis on the love rather
than the sovereignty of God. It in no way detracts from the nature
or the glory of God. One might say that it typifies the difference
between the Old Testament and the New Testament understandings
of God. Then the funeral becomes an instrument for glorifying
God because of his love and conveying that love to man in his
time of need. The love of God, like the love of man, provides a
climate of acceptance which is willing to permit and understand
the feelings of the individual. The mourner is given a picture of
God as one who will accept him in spite of the pain, perhaps even
bitterness, which he feels. He will recognize, if he has feelings of
guilt, that God is a loving and forgiving Father. He will come to
a better and more meaningful understanding of the Christian truth
that God is able to bring forth good out of evil, strength out of
pain, growth out of defeat. Much has been made in recent literature
of the place of love in therapy. Truly love is the therapy and the
therapy is love. This is as true in the divine as it is in the human
sense. Unless the mourner catches a vision of the love of God, a
severe impediment will be placed upon his willingness to mourn
genuinely.

Closely connected to this statement of the necessity to present the love of God is the need to explicate the nearness of God and his concern for his people. Christian theology never presents the nature of God without interpreting it in terms of his relationship to his people. Man was created to know God and live in fellowship with him. Such a statement becomes quite meaningless if one holds the complete otherness or transcendency of God. God is immanent as well as transcendent. He is at work in the world, in the universe in which we live, and in human experience. This implies that God is both willing and able to provide a source of strength to men in any crisis situation which may arise in their lives. In a sense the picture is one of God sharing the sorrow and suffering of the mourner—understanding it, seeking to provide relief from it. This makes it clear that mourning is not an act for which a man should feel ashamed, but that it is a way in which God enables him to grow beyond his loss.

Christian theology also contains a doctrine of man. It sees man as an individual of worth. The era of Rauschenbusch interpreted this rightly in terms of social worth, equality, and justice. Phychology offers an equally correct view of the worth of the individual in terms of selfhood and integrity. God's purpose for man includes the desire that man's personality or self should grow to fulfillment and integration, overcoming the personal afflictions and problems of life, among which we would include grief. Yet so often Christian pastors have misunderstood the very subtle distinction between selfishness and selfness. The Pauline and Augustinian theologies are correctly based upon the premise that the basis of sin is human selfishness and pride. Sin is man putting himself against God, stealing from God, seeking to usurp for himself the place of God. This is selfishness—that which man seeks for himself, for his own benefit, to the detriment of God or fellow men. Distinct from this is the concept of selfness, connoted as different from selfishness. Selfness is man's effort with the help of God to fulfill the divine purpose of his life by becoming a real self—whole, integrated, at peace with himself, God, and fellow men. Failing to apprehend this meaning of the concept of selfness, Christian

theology has at times cast out selfness along with selfishness as a
root of sin. The outgrowth of such an endeavor, if carried to its
logical conclusion, is either rigid asceticism or thoroughgoing
mysticism. Orthodox Protestant Christianity has gone to neither
of these extremes, although it has often held firmly to the premises
which would underlie such a position. To say that selfness, properly
considered, must have no place in Christian theology because it
is so easily perverted into selfishness is like saying that we must
have totalitarianism because individualism is so easily turned into
anarchy.

The Christian funeral has often been approached with the idea
that the intention is to take man's mind off himself and fix it on
God. This is to prevent man from pitying himself and to turn
him to the source of his strength. But this is only a half-truth.
The Christian funeral is to turn man's attention *to* himself and *to*
the resources which God offers for the strengthening and stabilizing
of the self. It has already been stated that bereavement creates a
crisis in life because it disorganizes the whole pattern of existence
and brings about a disintegration of the concept of the self. The
values of life and the purposes of life are shaken all out of focus.
A Christian faith and commitment offer the individual an opportunity to refocus his life around new purposes and values. The
simple expedient of finding purpose in meaningful Christian
service furnishes such a focus, provided it is not a compulsive
effort to escape from the painful reality of the situation of loss.

In all of these I have been thinking of faith and commitment
as a resource—a source of strength for meeting and working
through grief. The Christian faith enables individuals to mourn.
Yet so often Christian funerals have been conducted with the intention of substituting faith and hope for grief immediately. There
is serious danger in too easy reassurance. Faith is not a means of
escaping from the pain of grief, loss, and loneliness. It is a resource
which enables the faithful to endure and grow beyond these painful
experiences. It is an encouragement to mourn rather than a mandate
to sublimate grief. Kierkegaard and others have spoken of the leap
of faith. We can speak of it as the confidence and assurance of

the power and the love of God which enable us to plunge into a painful process of mourning in the sure and certain hope that we shall pass through to health and strength. As the leap of faith is taken, faith is strengthened and increased.

William Rogers offers a thought which provides an excellent climax to this section on the bases for theological criteria for judging the funeral.

When we have freed ourselves from the acute pain of the first loneliness and shock, then we are ready to enlarge our understanding of the meaning of life and death. Securing release from the pain of loss is not an act of disrespect to our loved one. It frees us for a more wholesome reverence. We are then ready to face and to understand the implications of our belief in immortality.[10]

A great deal of the substance of the funeral service and the customs which surround it is shaped by the aesthetic standards of the pastor and community. Undoubtedly this trend has been influenced very strongly by the rise of the professional funeral director. The function of the mortician has grown from one who prepared the body for burial to one who guides and directs a very large portion of the rites of the funeral. This is not to say that the funeral director issues orders to the minister, telling him how the service shall be conducted; his influence is far more subtle than that. His preparation of the body is augmented by a number of services offered to the family. This may include the furnishing of a funeral chapel, musicians, pallbearers, transportation, ordering flowers, making all necessary arrangements. In one way this is very helpful to the average family, which is faced with a strange situation at a time when it is very difficult to spend a great many hours making plans and decisions. At the same time it often gives rise to the establishment of standards which are gauged by smooth operation, sentimentality, and beauty, without any regard for the feelings of the mourners or their deep needs. A pattern is quickly developed in which efficiency and unctuousness become the *summa bona.*

[10] *Op. cit.,* p. 55.

While the morticians and other professional and commercial interests which have come to play a larger and larger part in the conduct of funeral services cannot be absolved completely for promoting many objectionable practices, in all fairness it should be recognized that many of their services are a result of the wishes of their clientele. They are following one of the laws of competitive business which demands that they provide all the services furnished by their competitors in addition to originating some services of their own. This easily develops into a vicious circle from which there is no other escape than mass re-education.

Many of the professional standards of the mortican have been voluntarily carried over into the church. Smoothness and beauty have become very real goals in the conduct of the funeral. This has been doubly emphasized in the idea which the church has often held that a Christian should face death and grief calmly and with composure. Many modern pastors have adopted one general criterion for determining what will and will not be in the funeral service. They have asked: Will it cause a display of emotion? Consequently they have ruled out music from the service because experience showed that so many people burst into tears during the funeral music. (This is not limited to some of the sentimental and theologically atrocious funeral ditties.) They have forbidden the family to view the body before leaving the church because this action was often accompanied by weeping and sobbing. They have striven to make sermons impersonal because a mention of the deceased sometimes brought forth an emotional reaction from the mourners. We must ask ourselves: What are the motives for this? One motivation is most certainly aesthetic. We prefer to have things done "decently and in order." We want the funeral, like any other service of worship, to be dignified, smooth, and effective. Therefore anything which mars the dignity and order of the service by a display of crude emotion is taboo.

Another motivation is misplaced pride on the part of the pastor. What minister has not at some time said to himself: "I worked hard in that funeral service and sermon to bring the comfort of Christian truth to these friends. But in spite of my assurances of

God's loving care, in spite of my efforts to instill the courage of faith, in spite of my presentation of the hope of the resurrection, still they wept. I have failed to comfort my people." So a subtle defensiveness takes over. The pastor, instead of realizing that a show of emotion does not necessarily betray a lack of faith and understanding, begins to remove from the service any things which have shown themselves to produce the reaction which he wants to avoid because it throws doubt upon the effectiveness of his ministry.

Still another motivation is embarrassment because of lack of empathy. We are often embarrassed by being in the presence of someone who is experiencing strong feeling which we ourselves do not feel. A third party is embarrassed by a display of affection between lovers, but the lovers are not embarrassed in each other's presence. The embarrassment connected with seeing someone suffer in bereavement is keen unless we have some of the same feeling within us. This does not mean that we can experience it with the same intensity that they feel. That is quite unlikely. Nevertheless if the pastor cannot accept, understand, and, in part, feel what the mourners are feeling, he will seek to avoid those factors in the funeral which contribute to his embarrassment.

There is one other motivation which might be called sympathy, as distinguished from empathy. When we see someone in pain, we become sympathetic and want to do everything we can to relieve his pain. When we see someone weeping, we want to help him stop the flow of tears and divert his mind to less painful thoughts. One can easily see how this would influence a pastor as he conducts a funeral. But we must bear in mind that sometimes the healing process is painful. The pain may be the impetus for seeking a cure. If the symptomatic pain is removed or masked, the disease may continue unimpaired.

We can add to this aesthetic desire for beauty and composure in the funeral a cultural dimension. In our culture a demonstration of emotion is often interpreted as a sign of weakness. This particular vestige of Victorianism has lingered much longer than most aspects of that era. We see composure and control as indications of strength and superiority. Perhaps we can see a very far-reaching implication of this in the way most white Americans smile at the so-called emotional excesses of a Negro or foreign funeral. We take refuge in the "superiority" of ritual and practices which are aesthetically smooth and unemotional.

There is a peculiar contradiction involved in this whole matter. By definition aesthetics are concerned with beauty, which has an emotional appeal. I have used aesthetics here to describe practices which appeal to only a part of the human emotions rather than the totality of feelings. In so doing, it is possible to stress artistic appreciation and the appeal of beauty to such an extent that other strong and potentially meaningful feelings are subverted. This would indicate that there are relevant values in the aesthetic aspects of the funeral, but that these values are reduced or destroyed when the aesthetic is considered in the narrow sense and used as an escape from the feelings of the whole person or when it becomes an end in itself.

Some of the psychological criteria which I propose have already been discussed. I have spoken of the denial of the reality of death. The funeral which has as its theme "There is no death" prevents the mourner from facing the fact of death. This poses a extremely perplexing problem for the bereaved. If the fact of death is denied, then why does he feel pain? He is faced with one of two choices: either he will become very confused because he has feelings for which there is no explanation, or he will deny and repress the feelings which are apparently baseless. I have already pointed out the psychological damage which can be brought about in this way.

In like fashion the funeral must provide a sense of finality. Mourning is a process which entails the breaking of ties with the deceased. The funeral may be looked upon as one of the beginning stages of that process. If it encourages a sense of unfinished business, as though death had not really occurred, difficulty will be encountered in the severing of these ties.

At the same time the funeral must be an aid in recalling memories of the past, thinking freely of the deceased. This may appear to be a contradiction of what has just been said about the breaking of ties. One might think that recalling the deceased would only serve to strengthen the ties. It would seem that forgetting the past would be a more effective *modus operandi*. The phrase "learning to live with the memory of the deceased," which is found in Lindemann and Rogers, indicates that freedom comes through assimilation rather than denial. Once the person is able to live comfortably with memories of the deceased, he has been able to adjust to his loss and is no longer bound in a morbid association with the one who has died. The funeral which fosters the beginning of this process has served the mourner well.

This carries us into another criterion for judging the effectiveness of the funeral from the standpoint of the bereaved. The funeral is to provide an atmosphere for the difficult work in mourning. There should be nothing in the funeral service which short-circuits or detours the mourning process. It should establish rapport for whatever assistance the minister may be able to give as the bereaved undertakes the work of mourning. It should indicate, not in academic psychological terminology, to be sure, the necessity for finding anew an integration in life. Lindemann writes:

Religious agencies have led in dealing with the bereaved. They have provided comfort by giving the backing of dogma to the patient's wish for continued interaction with the deceased, have developed rituals which maintain the patient's interaction with others, and have counteracted the morbid guilt-feelings of the patient by Divine Grace and by promising an opportunity for "making up" to the deceased at the time of a later reunion. While these measures have helped countless mourners, comfort alone does not provide adequate assistance in the patient's grief work. He has to review his relationships with the deceased, and has to become acquainted with the alteration in his own modes of emotional reaction. . . . He will have to express his sorrow and sense of loss. He will have to find an acceptable formulation of his future relationship to the deceased. He will have to verbalize his feelings of guilt, and he will have to find persons around him whom he can use as "primers" for the acquisition of new patterns of conduct.[11]

[11] *Op. cit.*, p. 147. Used by permission of the author and of the *American Journal of Psychiatry*.

Here is a psychiatrist giving his understanding of the psychological function of the funeral service of the church as it abets the mourning process in the bereaved. If we can accuse Lindemann of anything, it is his charity in reflecting upon the functioning of the church in situations of bereavement.

The final means I would suggest for judging the efficacy of the funeral is variability. I have sought to demonstrate that the impact and content of bereavement vary with every individual. Some feel confused, some feel guilty, some feel hostile, and so on. One cannot hope that the same funeral ritual and practice would fit every occasion and individual need. Therefore some degree of variability must be provided for. There are in Protestantism both liturgical churches and churches which espouse the practice of free worship; what I have to say here applies to both. Both types of services were originally designed to meet human need. Once they settled into a static form, either liturgical or free, the possibility of insensitivity to human need was greatly increased. The funeral must be guided and influenced by the needs of the mourner. While the general form of the funeral service may remain constant, the content of every funeral should seek to provide the help which is required by the particular individuals in their own situations. Every funeral, although it relates to the one central experience of death, must be a unique service which speaks to individuals. This variability is essential in making the funeral a meaningful experience.

The criteria for evaluating the effectiveness of the personal function of the funeral are:

1. The funeral must deal with death realistically.

2. The funeral must present a vision of God which will be of comfort and help to the mourners in their suffering. This includes the understanding of the love of God, the nearness of God, and his concern for his people.

3. The funeral must see man as an individual of worth, turning man's attention to the importance of his personal integration and the resources which God offers for the strengthening and stabilizing of the self.

4. The funeral must demonstrate that the Christian faith is a resource which enables the individual to mourn, rather than a substitute for mourning.

5. The funeral must recognize and accept deep feelings, rather than cover them up by a superficial aestheticism.

6. The funeral must provide a sense of finality.

7. The funeral must be an aid in recalling memories of the deceased.

8. The funeral is to establish a climate for mourning.

9. The funeral must be sensitive to the individual needs of the bereaved, dynamic, variable in both form and content.

CHAPTER FIVE

ELEMENTS OF THE FUNERAL SERVICE

WE TURN NOW to the application of the criteria which have been proposed for the funeral rituals and practices which are in current usage. No attempt is made to distinguish the theological, aesthetic, or psychological categories because they are bound in a whole. Their unity is found in the way in which they seek to meet human need in a manner which is both meaningful and beneficial to the bereaved.

The consideration of the ritual is based upon books of worship of a number of major Protestant denominations: *The Book of Common Prayer* of the Protestant Episcopal Church in the U.S.A., *The Book of Common Worship* of the Presbyterian Church in the U.S.A., *The Book of Worship* of the Evangelical and Reformed Church, *The Ritual of the Methodist Church*, *The Book of Church Order* of the Presbyterian Church in the U.S., as well as nondenominational funeral manuals, such as *Minister's Service Book* by J. D. Morrison, *A Service Book* edited by W. Halsey Smith, *The Pastor's Ideal Funeral Manual* edited by Nolan B. Harmon, Jr., *A Living Hope* by Jesse Halsey, and Andrew Blackwood's *The Funeral*. No effort is made to evaluate these books or the portions pertaining to the funeral as such. I shall deal only with representative selections to illustrate the way in which the funeral can best minister to the individual needs of the mourners.

The funeral service itself shall be examined in four segments: the ritual, the sermon, the music, and the committal service. These portions of the ritual are inevitably found in the Christian funeral service.

The ritualistic elements of the funeral most generally include two major divisions, the reading of the Scripture and prayers.

Scripture Readings

In seeking to evaluate this portion of the funeral service, there are several questions which we must ask: What is the purpose of reading passages from the Bible? What are the meaning and connotation of these passages for the bereaved? Is the imagery which is contained in the words significant in the experience of the mourners? Do the scripture passages speak to the particular needs of the mourners in this unique situation?

The purpose of reading selections from the Bible goes much deeper than a merely traditional practice or an effort to follow an established order of service. In the first place, it is a way in which the hope and comfort of the gospel is brought to bear upon a situation of human need. This should be understood in the light of what was said in the last chapter, that the Christian faith and hope are resources which enable people to mourn rather than ways in which the process of mourning can be displaced or thwarted. The verses and chapters from the Bible which are read at the funeral service should recognize the truth that those who mourn are comforted by their mourning. Second, the purpose of the reading of the Scripture is a means of demonstrating the way in which Christianity confronts the reality of death, its mystery and finality. Third, passages from the Bible can indicate to the mourner a deep understanding, recognition, and acceptance of his feelings. If he can find in the reading of the Word the same feelings which he is experiencing, he will not only be in a better position to understand himself but will also be enabled to rely on the resources of his religion because he sees that his feelings are understood. This threefold interpretation of the purpose for reading from the Scripture in the funeral service makes possible a much broader conception of the value of the application of biblical truth for improving the personal function of the funeral.

The second question we ask is: What are the meaning and connotation of these passages for the bereaved? We, the pastors of the churches, so often fall into error by supposing that our parishioners automatically attach the same significance and interpretation to verses of Scripture which we do as we read them. We forget that they do not have the advantage of seminary courses in Bible and systematic theology, or shelves of commentaries, or, perhaps, hours spent in reflecting upon the meaning of biblical material. Thus very often we evidence considerable naïveté in presenting passages of the Scripture, knowing what they mean to us but not asking what they mean to the man in the pew. We would be appalled by some of the tragic misinterpretations which are made by laymen because their pastor thought that everyone would see the meaning as he sees it himself. It is not enough to ask what a particular verse or passage means. We must ask what it means for the listeners.

We know that human needs exert a very definite influence upon perception. The ink blots of the Rorschach tests are interpreted in different ways by different individuals. The experienced tester can understand the needs of the individual by understanding what the ink blot means to him. It is impossible for the minister to be a psychological tester, but the underlying theory is applicable to the pastoral obligations. Every scripture reference used in the funeral must be subjected to the test: What will this mean to the mourners? For example, "I am the resurrection, and the life; he that believeth in me, though he were dead, yet shall he live; and whosoever liveth and believeth in me shall never die" (John 11:25-26). The beauty and truth of this passage are undeniable. But its applicability under certain circumstances is open to question. For example, what meaning will these words convey to an individual who is experiencing difficulty in accepting the fact that a loved one has really died, that the human relationships with the deceased are broken? Will the parishioner understand that this verse refers to spiritual rather than physical life and death? Will he find comfort in these words, or will they stimulate harmful confusion by providing a justification for escaping the fact of death with a supposed sanction of the church? Or take the familiar passage from Job, "The Lord gave, and the Lord hath taken away; blessed be the name of the Lord" (Job 1:21). A pastor has interpreted this verse to himself, recognizing that it does not make of God a sadistic tyrant, but rather is a description of the creative function of God and the natural result of mortality in the economy of God. But how does a father of several small children understand this verse as he sits at the side of his wife's casket? Will it turn him away from God in bitterness? Will it make him feel guilty and estranged from God because he should bless the name of the Lord but cannot bring himself to do it? Will it thrust him into a spirit of utter resignation to a blind fate? The pastor must try with all earnestness and keenness of insight to see the way in which the Scripture will be understood by the mourner.

In questioning the appropriateness of certain scripture passages, as we are doing in this chapter, we should understand that it is not the truth or validity of the verses which is being questioned, but the feasibility of using them in a situation which does not permit adequate interpretation or which is so loaded with feeling that the obvious meaning in relation to the situation will be jumped at unreflectively and uncritically. The passage from Job which was mentioned above is a part of almost every standard funeral ritual. It undoubtedly is a valid statement. But it would seem to be much more appropriate for a Sunday-morning sermon when it could be fully explored and interpreted than for a funeral service where needy people will grasp at its surface meaning and be thrust from God rather than drawn to him.

In connection with the meaning which people give to the scripture passages we also must examine the imagery which is used. The eternal value of the Bible is dimmed if people do not comprehend the imagery and word pictures which it contains. We must be realistic in admitting that we live in a generation which is biblically illiterate. People do not possess the vocabulary or thought forms to make sense of a good deal of the Scripture. This is a tragedy, but we do not reduce its tragic consequences by denying the existence of the problem. One effort to counter this situation is seen in the modern translations of the Bible which are renewing the Reformation emphasis on translations into the vernacular. There is some truth in the statement made by Blackwood:

As a rule the best version for use at a funeral is the King James Version. While it has minor flaws, the language is notable for beauty. Even the prose has a pleasing rhythm. The diction has a dignity and elevation rarely found in recent translations. The fact that the old version is familiar makes it welcome in the time of sorrow. That is when the heart cries out for the old faith and the familiar landmarks, as they appear in mother's Bible.[1]

There are some passages, such as Ps. 23 or John 14, in which this is most certainly true. But for others, such as I Cor. 15, a modern biblical illiterate may find a great deal more meaning in the language and imagery of the Revised Standard Version.

We must also remember that the picture of God which is sometimes presented in the Old Testament is quite different from that of the gospel. Compare, for example, "For we are consumed by thine anger, and by thy wrath are we troubled" (Ps. 90:7), with, "(Nothing) shall . . . separate us from the love of God, which is in Christ Jesus" (Rom. 8:39b). The imagery contained in such passages obviously can have a very important bearing upon the value of the funeral for the individual.

Then, too, we must examine the appropriateness of the scripture verses for recognizing and dealing with the needs of the individual. Here, once again, the pastor must try to see the needs as the mourner himself feels them. Does he feel lonely, confused, fearful, guilty, resentful? The appropriateness of the scripture readings will spell the difference between a helpful or a harmful experience for him in the funeral. It would be impossible to explore this subject exhaustively. Let me illustrate it with one of the more extreme situations, recognizing that the same pattern which is shown here carries over into every situation. In Chapter III I described the bereavement of Mr. and Mrs. Lewis, whose little daughter was killed by fractious cattle which they had put off selling. They recognized their responsibility, although it was indirect, and experienced strong guilt feelings. Note the difference which the selection of scripture readings could make in the possibility of therapy taking place in the funeral. Suppose that the pastor chose to read,

[1] *Op. cit.*, p. 100.

"Thou hast set our iniquities before thee, our secret sins in the light of thy countenance" (Ps. 90:8), and, "When thou with rebukes dost correct man for iniquity, thou makest his beauty to consume away like a moth; surely every man is vanity" (Ps. 39:11), and, "If thou, Lord, shouldest mark iniquities, O Lord, who shall stand?" (Ps. 130:3), and, "For we must all appear before the judgment seat of Christ; that every one may receive the things done in his body, according to that he hath done, whether it be good or bad" (II Cor. 5:10).

Perhaps the pastor did not single out these verses as I have done here, but he took his funeral manual and read a number of selections from it in which these passages just happened to be. Or perhaps he felt that it was his responsibility to secure conviction of sin in order that through repentance forgiveness might be received. In any case the net result of such a funeral not only would deepen any sense of guilt which existed, but would compound the difficulty of mourning.

Suppose, on the other hand, that the pastor chose to read, "Hear, O Lord, when I cry with my voice: have mercy also upon me, and answer me" (Ps. 27:7), and, "I will lift up mine eyes unto the hills; from whence cometh my help" (Ps. 121:1), and, "Let not your heart be troubled: ye believe in God, believe also in me" (John 14:1), and, "Like as a father pitieth his children, so the Lord pitieth them that fear him" (Ps. 103:13). It should be understood that these few verses will not relieve at once the feelings of guilt which the parents have. But two constructive things may occur as a result of such an approach. First, no effort is made to draw attention to or away from guilt feelings, creating an atmosphere of free acceptance rather than judgment. Second, reference is made to God as the resource of strength for any difficulty, as a sympathetic Father, as one who stands ready to understand man's deepest feelings. In this way there is an opportunity to lay the foundation for the work of mourning and the ultimate relief of guilt feelings in a sense of forgiveness.

In situations in which hostility is manifest biblical passages implying that death has come as the result of the will of God are par-

ticularly damaging. A person of mature faith may be able to assimilate the understanding of the will of God as interpreted, for example, by Leslie Weatherhead.[2] But under the pressure of malignant
resentment such an understanding is highly improbable. We know
that very often the hostility which is felt against the deceased is
projected on other individuals because the person does not feel
right about being angry with someone whom he should hold in
loving memory. To imply that the death is a result of the will of
God is virtually an invitation to project the hostility upon God.
This will make itself manifest either in a terrible bitterness which
alienates the individual from a source of strength and growth or
in a deeper sense of guilt because he has turned in anger upon both
the Deity and his loved one.

A great many of the passages of Scripture which are commonly
associated with funeral services stress the vanity of life. "Behold,
thou hast made my days as an handbreadth; and mine age is as
nothing before thee; verily every man at his best state is altogether
vanity" (Ps. 39:5.) "Thou carriest them away as with a flood;
they are as a sleep: in the morning they are like grass which groweth
up. In the morning it flourisheth, and groweth up; in the evening
it is cut down, and withereth" (Ps. 90:5-6.) "Man that is born of a
woman is of few days, and full of trouble." (Job 14:1.) "For
he knoweth our frame; he remembereth that we are dust" (Ps.
103:14.) These are illustrations of such passages. They are true
statements. Their original intention was to glorify God by por-
traying his strength against the background of human life. But
we must ask ourselves, without questioning the validity of
the statements themselves: How appropriate or beneficial are they
for a person whose life has been thrown into confusion, whose
self is disorganized by his loss? Their impact upon a confused
mourner would do more to accent the chaotic condition of his life,
instead of to fulfill their intended purpose of augmenting the view
of the glory of God.

It is very difficult to find passages which make an explicit interpretation of the meaning of death. But there are a number of

---

[2] *The Will of God* (New York and Nashville: Abingdon-Cokesbury Press, 1944).

chapters and verses which, at least implicitly, present the fact of the finality and reality of physical death, as well as the Christian understanding of the resurrection. However, many of these passages are couched in involved language which requires interpretation for most people of our generation. I Cor. 15, which is part of most standard rituals, is one of the best examples of this. In this chapter the contrast between the physical and spiritual life is made quite apparent. Mortality is presented as a fact. "For as in Adam all die, even so in Christ shall all be made alive" (I Cor. 15:22.) "For this perishable nature must put on the imperishable" (I Cor. 15:53 R.S.V.) In the same way the resurrection is explained, not as a denial of the fact of death or a means of explaining away the loss, but as a sure and certain hope of the new quality of life into which man is translated. Such passages, when they are properly interpreted in language and imagery which people can understand, can be very helpful to the mourner because they offer an explanation and understanding of the loss which he has suffered, thereby providing an explanation for his feelings in bereavement and also hope of resurrection, which offers the possibility of future interaction with the deceased.

The mourning process is aided by those passages which describe the nearness of God and his loving concern for human needs. Ps. 23, John 14, the closing verses of Rom. 8, Ps. 46, and many others fit into this category. In these sections, not only is there a presentation of the resources of strength which God offers, but, equally important, there is the recognition that man's situation is one of need. Properly interpreted, this should enable the bereaved to engage in mourning with the confidence that it is a perfectly natural process and that the therapeutic resources of God are at work in him.

The assertions which have been made concerning the various kinds of scripture passages which can be used in the funeral and their suitability in specific situations lead to the proposal that the selection of biblical material for the funeral service demands full concentration upon the presenting situation and the interpretation of the material on the basis of the needs of the mourners. We have

advanced beyond the stage when it could be said that certain scripture passages were for funerals. Even the selections given in books
of worship and funeral manuals were presumed to be applicable
to almost any funeral. Unfortunately this is not the case. If we are
to provide maximum assistance to the bereaved, we cannot see
their need only in terms of a universal or generalized pattern. We
have to interpret their needs individually and conduct the funeral
accordingly.

Thus it would seem much more realistic to prepare the scripture readings for a funeral by selecting verses which we understand
as being able to speak to the needs of the mourners in this situation.
I propose the use of verses rather than chapters because so often in
the same psalm or chapter a great variety of thoughts may be
contained, some of them helpful, others harmful, in the particular
situation. It will be a great deal more work for the pastor to select
a number of verses which pertain to the situation rather than to
decide to read the first three and the last passage in his service book.
But it will not only assure a more relevant and beneficial selection;
it will also stimulate the pastor to do some very serious thinking
about the dynamics which are involved in this particular case.

Prayers

A great deal of what has been said in this evaluation of the
scripture readings can be carried over into the analysis of the
other major portion of the ritual, the prayers. Once again my basic
premise is that the prayers should recognize and deal with the
needs which are felt by the mourners. This does not mean that
they must be "free prayers." They may be selected from a prayer
book. In either case the prayers must be carefully thought through
and evaluated by the criteria which have been suggested. Because
of the uniqueness of each individual mourning situation many
pastors will find that the use of carefully prepared *original prayers*
will be the most effective means of making the prayers relevant to
the mourners' experience.

The fact that I place major emphasis upon the subjective aspect
of prayer is determined by the nature of this discussion and is not

in any sense a denial of the objective validity of prayer. The psychological value of prayer has sometimes been seen as the inducing of a desired response. While this is undoubtedly true, it would also seem that the prayer may be a means of educing the feelings and responses of the individual. We cannot set the minister up as an omniscient seer who diagnoses the case of the mourner and then dispenses the proper pill to bring about the desired result. This appears to be the logical conclusion of a psychological theory of prayer which sees it only as a means for inducing a desired response. The whole funeral has a desired response, that of enabling the individual to mourn and be comforted; but I believe that this purpose will not be achieved by forcing the person into the proper pattern. Rather it is accomplished by providing an atmosphere in which the feelings of the individual may come out and be dealt with.

The prayers which are normally used in funeral rituals fall into three major categories: prayers of thanksgiving, prayers of confession, and prayers of intercession.

Although prayers of thanksgiving center around the goodness of God, they have a very definite point of contact with human experience as well. If they are to be at all meaningful, they must have a foundation in fact—in the experience and feeling of the mourners. Here is where the real danger of attempting to induce a response may be shown. If the minister gives thanks for those things for which the mourners do not feel at all grateful, what will be the effect of the prayer on their thinking? Will it induce thankfulness, or will it present a forbidding and hostile vision of God? Take, for example, a situation in which the prayer of thanksgiving includes an expression of gratitude that the end of life has given surcease from the afflictions of pain and suffering. For some people this would be a most meaningful prayer experience. For others, who did not possess a mature perspective, it would have a quite different result. The minister must bear in mind that he is not praying in the services of the church as an interceding priest but as a representative of the worshiping congregation. He has the responsibility to pray in such a way that the congregation can be praying along with him. The feelings of the worshipers must receive just as much consideration as the feelings of the one who is verbalizing the prayer. In using prayers of thanksgiving, the purpose of the pastor is to express thanks for those things for which the people are thankful, not to pray in order that they may feel grateful for favors received.

Keeping this in mind, let us look at some of the things for which thanks are given in most of the funeral rituals. In studying the prayers of thanksgiving in various services, we find that the things most often mentioned are expressions of gratitude for life and its potentialities, memories of the deceased and the good example of his life, the comfort and support of the promises of God contained in the Scripture, and the Christian hope in the life everlasting. The validity of such prayers of thanksgiving is without question, and the atmosphere which they provide can be conducive to the mourning process.

However, such prayers cannot be sown broadcast without any knowledge of the dynamics of the situation of the mourners. We can see how very easy it would be to stir up feelings of guilt and self-recrimination by ill-advised use of such prayers. Thanksgiving for the good example set by the deceased may be very helpful to some people as an aid in recalling memories of the dead, thereby abetting the work of mourning. But that same prayer may create a real problem for a mourner who has ambivalent feelings toward the deceased. Reminder of the good example of the deceased may only serve to stimulate a deep sense of guilt. The person may think: "I should be able to think a lot of good things about John too, but I just can't do it. What is the matter with me?" Or such an experience may throw up a very real obstacle against the establishment of rapport with the pastor: "He certainly doesn't understand things. He is saying all these good things about John, but he doesn't know how selfish John was."

In the same way prayers of thanksgiving for the comfort and strength of God's promises and the resources of the Christian faith can be misunderstood. People may get the idea that they are not supposed to mourn, unless the promises of God are interpreted to them as sources of strength for mourning rather than denials of the need for mourning. Our thankfulness is truly centered about the willingness of God to provide therapy through mourning.

Prayers of confession are very seldom explicit in the funeral service. Usually they are couched in general terms of human frailty and weakness rather than sinfulness. Those who have suggested the use of prayers of confession in the funeral have based their proposals on the place of sin at the roots of human suffering and misery. Death has been interpreted as the result of sin, sorrow as the burden of sin. Thus the inclusion of confession in the funeral is expected in some sense to mitigate the suffering. This view is both false and true. If physical mortality is seen as the wages of sin, there is little point in having confession, for death has already occurred. If all sorrow and suffering are seen as the wages of sin, then mourning must be evil and abnegated by confession. These assumptions are false.

But I have spoken of guilt feelings which are sometimes connected with the grief reaction. What value do prayers of confession have for such feelings? At first one would be inclined to say that they would be the ideal solution to the problem. But upon reflection one sees that a perfunctory or ill-timed confession is not permanently helpful. If the individual is not ready to engage in the introspective activity involved in confession, it may only deepen the sense of guilt and complicate the mourning process. It would seem far better to avoid formalized confession in favor of a presentation of the picture of God as one who stands ready to forgive man. Then the groundwork is laid for both divine acceptance and self-acceptance.

The majority of funeral prayers are intercessory, prayers for the meeting of the needs of the bereaved. Most service books contain a wide variety of such prayers. According to the criteria which have been proposed, some types of these prayers have positive value, while others appear to have a negative effect. Because of the large number of these prayers I shall speak in a categorical sense rather than attempt to cite specific examples.

The types of petitions which are helpful in achieving the goal of fulfilling human needs in the funeral are varied in content, but they have one common focus. They are those which seek God's help for the process of therapeutic mourning. Prayers for help in mourning emphasize the nearness and availability of God, asserting the resources which God offers to the mourners in their suffering. They recognize the painfulness of the situation and do not attempt to disguise its bitterness. Such prayers demonstrate an understanding of the feelings of the individuals on more than a superficial level. They do not present mourning as a burden which will be taken from the shoulders of the bereaved by God but speak of it as a human function for which the strength and resources of God are available. While they may ask God's help to bear the weight of grief, they do not assume that the individual has only to turn over his burden to God. In this way they make it clear that mourning is a very necessary task for the bereaved, presenting the Christian faith as a resource for working through grief but not a way of avoiding it.

Some intercessory prayers refer to the need for remembering the deceased. These, too, can have a very beneficial effect in fostering the process of mourning because they encourage the bereaved to think of the deceased instead of seeking to avoid pain by ruling every painful memory out of consciousness.

Some service books also contain prayers which encourage the assimilation of the experience of bereavement by seeking a new commitment of life. If this is presented in such a way that it does not become a compulsive means of escaping from the painful experience of mourning, it can be extremely helpful. It symbolizes the need for finding a new orientation and organization of life without the presence of the one who has died.

Some types of intercessory prayers, if judged by these criteria, have a negative effect upon mourning. Among these are prayers which ask for a spirit of resignation and submission to the will of God, which acknowledge this particular death as a direct result of God's causation. Not only is there some reason to question such assertions on theological grounds, but also we can say that they present an understanding of God as arbitrary or wrathful. This is not conducive then to picturing God as one who offers aid in mourning. In the same way prayers which urge submission to

God carry with them the connotation that, as has been said above, all that is required of man is that he place his burden upon God. Thus it becomes a very effective way of misinterpreting the real significance and function of mourning. Much in this same vein there are other prayers which make the easy assumption that faith is a substitute for mourning. Although we recognize that faith is one of the sources of strength for coming through the mourning process, this thought can hardly be conveyed in a prayer which assumes that if we have faith right now, we shall be comforted right now. Mourning is an extended process. If it is believed that a single step at the moment will remove the painfulness of suffering bereavement, there may be momentary relief. But when the process, which has not really been worked through, reasserts itself, the individual will think: "What's wrong? My faith must not be strong enough because I still feel like weeping." Instead of helping the person, an oversimplified view of the release from mourning only complicates his problem.

There is another type of intercessory prayer which is not too commonly used in many Protestant churches—the prayers for the dead. By this is not meant prayers for the improvement of the spiritual condition of the deceased or special favors for them. Their real theme appears to be a spirit of dedication. They may have significance to the mourners in the way in which they present the faith in the resurrection life, the possibility of future interaction with the deceased in later life. In a sense they also provide an accent to the fact that death has brought an entirely different relationship. The physical presence is no longer in evidence; that relationship has terminated because we now speak of them in the presence of God.

George Buttrick says:

Protestantism has suffered because, in proper recoil from arbitrary theories of purgatory, it has erased from prayer the memory and mention of the "communion of saints." The claims of spiritualism are often not spiritual, but earthbound. It would be strange if loved ones gone should communicate with friends on earth through mediums previously unknown. Even were the claims proved, we might well hesitate to ask "those on before" to talk to us by sound and sense—in terms of this world's life. But we believe there is an open way between the worlds: they are both in God's keeping. We believe in communion—through the better language of love and prayer, which both worlds speak and understand. Therefore we pray, privately and corporately, for the dead. Their world is hidden; and prayer therefore gropes. But the groping is in light, not in darkness. The language is baffled, but radiant. Such prayer penetrates another world, fulfills our love, comforts our sadness, and is worthy of him in whom our faith dwells.[3]

The Lord's Prayer is included in many funeral services. Without in any way noting the evident significance and value of the content of this prayer in all the circumstances of life, including bereavement, we can see an additional value in its use. The Lord's Prayer is customarily prayed in unison. Its use in the funeral service provides an opportunity for a joining of the spirits of the bereaved and their friends in united supplication to God. It is an effective way of witnessing to the unity of the fellowship and its meaning in such a time of crisis.

Prose and Poetry Selections

Another part of the funeral service is the inclusion of prose selections and poetry. None of the denominational books of worship make provision for the use of this type of literature, but a number of funeral source books have rather extensive selections of material which can be used in the service. In spite of the fact that it is not included in the classic form of the ritual, the quotation of prose or poetry has found its way into many modern funerals.

There can be a definite value in the use of literary quotations. The rich experiences of others who have gone through bereavement and undergone the process of mourning can be shared with the mourners at the funeral. There is no reason why the words of the poet or author cannot contain a theologically and psychologically adequate statement of the meaning of death and the significance of mourning. But such selections must be tested against the same criteria which have been applied to the rest of the service.

[3] *Prayer*, p. 276. Copyright 1942 by Whitmore & Stone. Used by permission of Abingdon-Cokesbury Press.

Unfortunately so many of the poetic resources which are offered in funeral manuals either are characterized by a gushy sentimentalism or are attempts to deny the reality of death through euphemisms. While we make no effort to pronounce the judgment of literary criticism on these works, we are quite sure that they would not stand in the critic's court. We can find sufficient evidence to secure conviction on psychological grounds alone. Some of the most objectionable poetry from this standpoint centers around a misguided effort to deny the reality of death. I have already spoken of the damage which this can cause to the mourner. Yet at so many funerals a well-meaning pastor will read poetry to the effect that there is no death, it is only an illusion; that the deceased is not really dead, he is only on a journey into the unknown; that there is nothing in death which hurts because it is just passing through a garden gate. Words such as these, if they are taken seriously by the bereaved, are bound to create a great deal of confusion in his thinking. If death is not real, why is his loved one gone, why does he feel sad and upset, why should he mourn?

A great deal of the poetry commonly selected for funerals falls into the pattern of what we discussed in the last chapter as an effort to cover up deep feelings with a superficial aesthetic appeal. It is not the beauty of prose or poetry which assuages pain, but the sharing of a deep experience by the poet and his reader or hearer. This is true because the former is an attempt to remove grief by displacing it with sweetness and light, while the latter is a means of aiding the mourner to think through his own experience under the stimulus of thinking of the similar experience of the writer.

The Funeral Sermon

One possible reason for the increasing use of poetry in funeral services is the discontinuation in many communities of the practice of preaching a funeral sermon. The reasons for this discontinuation are several. Blackwood sees it this way:

Doubtless because such a message in the past has not always been well prepared and properly delivered. Often it has been too long, too trite, too dull. It has seemed conventional, lifeless, impractical. In the worst sense of the word, the funeral sermon has been otherworldly.[4]

We could add to this the modern trend to make of the funeral a thing of aesthetic beauty in order to avoid the expression of deep feelings rather than a meaningful experience. This is closely associated with the mass production techniques which have crept in through the professionalism which characterizes many modern funerals. The smooth operations of the funeral director, the secular atmosphere of the mortuary chapel, the spiritual and literary mediocrity of a great many funeral sermons in the past, along with the fact that the preparation and delivery of a funeral sermon is one of the most difficult tasks for a pastor, have conspired to reduce the frequency of the use of sermons in the modern funeral.

This is a great tragedy, for the funeral sermon is one of the finest opportunities which the minister has to open the door for the fulfillment of the mourning process. I have alluded to the number of passages from the Scripture which require interpretation in the light of our understanding of grief and the way in which our faith can enable us to meet it. Where except in the sermon does the pastor have the chance to offer such interpretation?

Perhaps this will become more apparent if we inquire into the purpose of the funeral sermon. There have been many reasons in the past for preaching at the funeral. Sometimes the funeral sermon was viewed as one of the greatest evangelistic opportunities for the pastor. Many people who did not regularly attend church worship services came to funerals. So the pastor sought to present the challenge of the gospel to them while he had the chance. This, compounded with a view of death as judgment, provided a real crisis situation for the preaching of an evangelistic sermon. Funeral sermons were designed to take advantage of opportunities to lead men to a sense of conviction and repentance. By reminding people that their own lives were short, an appeal was made for conversion. Fortunately this approach to the funeral sermon has been discontinued in most parts of the country and in most major denominations.

[4] Op. cit., p. 135.

Its place was taken by another understanding of the reason for the funeral sermon, that of strengthening the faith of individuals so that they would no longer mourn but bravely stand amid the storm. This was a half step in the right direction. At least it began to focus attention on the mourners themselves and their needs. The error was made in a fallacious understanding of what the mourners needed. It was believed, as has been said several times, that if you could in some way strengthen a man's faith, it would displace his grief. Sermons were used to present the Christian hope, but in such a way that the bereaved were virtually compelled not to mourn lest they indicate weakness in their faith. While this purpose was well intentioned, it missed the real meaning of mourning and the relationship of faith to it. It was a positive approach exclusively. It wanted people to think of life rather than death, of joy rather than sorrow, of strength rather than weakness. But psychotherapy has shown in many ways that the recognition and acceptance of negative feelings as well as positive are essential to the therapeutic process. The funeral which fails to take into consideration the negative feelings of the individual, in this instance the painful experience of mourning, can accomplish very little of therapeutic value.

Therefore I propose a third purpose for the funeral sermon. It offers an opportunity to present a realistic view of death, an understanding of the feelings of the individual, an interpretation of the resources of the Christian faith as they relate to human needs. The sermon offers to the pastor a means of being of help to the mourners by indicating his understanding of their feelings which is unsurpassed by any other portion of the service. This does not mean that the pastor must deliver a sermon of great length. A short message of ten minutes or less, focusing on one or two central ideas, should accomplish the important ministry which is offered to the bereaved in this portion of the funeral service. Virtually all the criteria which have been suggested for the funeral can be applied in the sermon, making it a beneficial and meaningful experience for the mourners.

The sermon is one of the most variable portions of the funeral service. Since its content is not prescribed by any ritualistic pattern, it can be varied easily to suit the individual needs represented in each situation. The subject to be dealt with is always the same, the meaning of life and death; but the application of the subject is open to infinite variety. By relating the sermon to the human needs of the mourners the monotony of standardization can easily be avoided.

There has in recent years been an appeal to preaching which is associated with the life situation. When this has been applied to the funeral sermon, it has most often been related to the life of the deceased. The type of funeral sermon which I propose is related to the life situation of the mourners. There has been hesitancy on the part of pastors to preach life-situation funeral sermons because they have felt that to speak of the life of the deceased would either slip into the pattern of eulogizing, or it would place them in an awkward position if they were called upon to preach a funeral sermon for a person whose character or actions did not make good sermon material. They feared the day when they would be called upon to preach a life-situation sermon for the community reprobate or a suicide. Therefore it was much safer to make a general policy of keeping funeral sermons away from the specifics of life and focusing upon spiritual generalities.

I am suggesting that the funeral sermon be focused on the life situation of the mourners rather than the deceased. The problem of preaching oneself into a compromising situation then becomes much less critical. Just as we have often mouthed the cliché that funerals are for the living and not for the dead, we can say that funeral sermons are to be focused on the living and not on the dead.

This does not mean that we have to keep any mention of the deceased from the funeral sermon. Quite the opposite is true. It is a very helpful thing to mention in the funeral sermon the deceased, his life, and his activities. This is not an appeal for a return to eulogies. Its relevance to the situation is seen in the way it recognizes that the deceased has been a very important part of the lives of the mourners. It assists them in recalling memories of the deceased, which are, as I have indicated, a part of the mourning process. Instead of urging people to forget, as though the deceased had never lived, it sanctions the useful function of such memories. The pastor does not have to wax eloquent about the virtues of the deceased nor unduly praise him. But he does have a responsibility to make manifest in some way the fact that a life which has been an important focus in the experience of the mourners has been meaningful to them, that the relationship as they have known it is now ended, and that their memories of the deceased can be an important factor in the lessening of their pain.

The sermon can also be helpful as it witnesses to the fact that in the funeral service, the kindnesses of friends, and the fellowship of the Christian community there is an opportunity for the sharing of sorrow and loss. This sharing cannot be overemphasized or sentimentalized to the point that people think: "How can friends and neighbors feel as deeply about Mother's death as we do?" Such an impression cuts off the value that can be found in the sharing of sorrow. Far better to make it perfectly clear that the loss incurred through death pains the most when it is closest to us, but that there is still a sense of sadness and loss for those who were less intimately associated with the deceased because they, too, have lost a meaningful part of their pattern of life. The sharing of sorrow is more an understanding and acceptance of the feelings of the mourners than an attempt to equal the depth of their feelings.

If the sermon is related to the experiences of the mourners, it also has to take into consideration the possibility of the various types of complications of morbid or distorted reactions. These feelings may not be fully developed or evident at the time of the funeral, but that does not relieve the pastor of his responsibility to be sensitive to their possibility. In cases where he has good cause to believe that such feelings exist, his sermon should reflect that understanding. He can recognize the possibility of negative feelings in human relationships and demonstrate both the human and the divine understanding of such feelings. This does not mean that he should make verbal recognition of the fact, lest he be guilty of embarrassing the bereaved ones by suggesting in the presence of the congregation that their feelings have some undesirable aspects. However, he can interpret mourning in such a way that the persons will see the relationship of their feelings to the mourning process. For example, under such circumstances a minister might be able to make an interpretaton of Isa. 66:13, "As one whom his mother comforteth, so will I comfort you," a very helpful and therapeutic experience. Of course this would be a most disastrous selection if the mourner felt hostile toward his deceased mother. The idea which could be brought out of such a text in other circumstances would be an analogy between the divine love which accepts us and the love of a mother which is accepting in both the ups and downs of life, the positive and the negative aspects of human existence.

It is not extreme to suggest that just as funeral manuals contain long lists of sermon suggestions for various types of people who have died—mothers, children, aged, church officers, sufferers, and so on—it should be possible to conceive a number of sermon themes which approach the funeral sermon in terms of various types of mourners and the needs which are represented in their lives.

The connection of the funeral sermon to the mourning process which continues after the funeral can be strengthened by following the practice of some pastors who in the first call after the funeral give copies of their sermon to members of the family. If the sermon is such that it is related to the therapy of mourning, this policy will be of significant worth in demonstrating that the funeral is not an isolated experience but an integral part of the mourning process.

Music

Another part of most funeral services which should receive our attention in this evaluation is the selection and performance of music. This is a source of concern for many pastors. This problem is colored by a great number of factors. Much of the music which is commonly considered to be "funeral music" is obnoxious on both theological and aesthetic or artistic grounds. The heart, not to mention the stomach, of many a pastor has turned within him at the dolorous renditions of "Going Down the Valley One by One," "In the Sweet By and By," and "Beautiful Isle of Somewhere." By no stretch of the theological, aesthetic, or psychological imagination can a place be found for this sort of lugubrious music. The church and the ministry are entirely correct in reacting against it.

Sometimes all funeral music, even of the much higher types, is opposed on the grounds that it is emotional and sets off a reaction in the mourners. It is considered to be bad solely on the grounds that it brings tears to the eyes of the mourners. This in itself need not be bad. While it is true that a pastor does not deliberately set out to make people react emotionally by weeping at a funeral, we cannot say that he must avoid such a reaction at any cost. In that case the whole funeral could be made much more pleasant and unemotional by preaching on the world situation or missions, completely ignoring the fact that there are deep emotions or feelings involved in the service. If the emotional reactions of the mourners are properly interpreted and channeled, they can be shown to be of benefit rather than detriment.

Another way of approaching the problem of funeral music is to propose that it be limited to the great hymns of the church. This is justifiable so long as hymns are not selected solely on the basis of being great hymns, regardless of their implications in the particular situation. For example, "What a Friend We Have in Jesus" is a well-loved hymn in much of Protestantism. But consider the implication of one of its early lines, "All our sins and griefs to bear." If the mourner is listening thoughtfully to these words, do they present an accurate picture of the mourning through which he must go to find peace, or is it an encouragement to think, "God will take care of it," and then devote his time to avoiding his own mourning work? The selection of hymns should be made under the same evaluative criteria which are applied in this entire chapter.

In some communities members of the family often suggest hymns for the service. This is partly an administrative problem and partly a problem of the ministry to the bereaved. Administratively the pastor has the right and obligation to maintain his own integrity by tactfully rejecting selections of hymns which are theologically incorrect, aesthetically inappropriate, or psychologically harmful. It may be well for him to explain his reasons for objecting to the family's choice of music, thus giving him an excellent opportunity to interpret the meaning of Christian mourning to them. However, if the selections are within the limits of the standards mentioned above, on psychological grounds there may be real benefit in allowing the family to make a selection. They will undoubtedly select hymns which are meaningful to them, thus presenting a two-fold advantage: such selections are excellent indications of the needs which they feel and also represent a way of meeting those needs. There is also the possibility that the hymns which they select will be favorites of the deceased. In the hearing of these hymns they will once again be confronted with an opportunity to remember the deceased. This may bring tears, but in the psychological evaluation it is worth it.

There is yet another advantage which can be secured in the funeral music. This is found in the congregational singing of hymns, a practice which is not widely enough practiced today. The singing of hymns, selected on the bases suggested above, is helpful in giving a feeling of solidarity in the united action of the fellowship in singing. It symbolizes the sharing of sorrow by the entire community in the service. It enables the congregation to make a contribution to the service and the meaning which is symbolized in it by participating in the service.

The Committal Service

The last part of the actual funeral service which I shall examine is the committal service. This is usually a rather brief service (with the exception of the one in the *Book of Common Prayer*) which is the concluding portion of the funeral. It is an extremely difficult time for the mourners because it represents the time when they leave the body of their loved one in the grave. There is an element of completeness and finality in this moment, and in this we find one of its major psychological values. The committal service provides, as nothing else in the funeral does so graphically, a symbolic demonstration that the kind of relationship which has existed between the mourner and the deceased is now at an end. This experience as it is reflected upon in the process of mourning enables the person to understand the necessity for the reorientation of life around a new focus. Unless the finality of death is understood in this sense, there will be a very real impediment to adjustment.

This experience as it is reflected upon in the process of mourning Christian doctrine of the resurrection which is also symbolized in the committal service. The fact of burial does not detract from the belief that the life of the spirit is renewed. I have already commented upon the psychological significance of the belief in the resurrection.

Both of these elements should be in the committal service and should be interpreted as much as possible. The service should not focus only upon the body and spirit of the deceased, but also upon the needs of the mourners. This latter consideration is quite often omitted from the standard committal service. The scripture selections, prayers, and the statement of dedication or committal refer to the deceased. Only in a few of the prayers are there references to the needs of the individuals.

It is very difficult to deny the reality of death in a committal service. Although the majority of the references are to the life of the spirit, the symbolically significant action has to do with the burial of the body. In this action, painful though it may be, there is help for the individual.

The reason for burial or cremation is to allow the body to disintegrate. This dissolution of the body involves the dissolution of human relationships as well. Thus it has a very definite psychological significance in stimulating the realization that old relationships are gone and new relationships must be formed. The committal and burial, or cremation, should convey this sense of completion of the human phase of existence. There should be no sense of unfinished business or unsevered relationships. This may sound very heartless, but so long as a person denies in any way that the deceased is really gone, he will remain in bondage to the deceased.

My treatment of the committal is limited to this particular action of burial. Anything which might be said in evaluation of the biblical passages or prayers would be subsumed under the discussion of those elements of the funeral service earlier in this chapter.

This analysis of the funeral service has been made, not with the intention of iconoclasm, but in the hope that the unity of the theological, aesthetic, and psychological principles which shape the service may be recognized. These principles work together to demonstrate the sensitivity of the funeral to human needs and to proffer the resources of the Christian faith which make possible the meeting of those needs.

CHAPTER SIX

FUNERAL PRACTICES

WHEN WE SPEAK of the funeral, we are not only discussing the religious service which takes place in the church or the mortuary. The concept of the funeral includes a great many customs and practices which are not a part of the service by inclusion in the ritual but which have come to be almost universally associated with the funeral in our culture.

In dealing with the practices and customs which accompany the funeral, I have relied upon information which has been gathered from personal experience, conversations with fellow pastors, funeral manuals mentioned in the preceding chapter, and small brochures on the funeral which have been prepared by several pastors for distribution among their parishioners. These include *When Death Comes* by W. Thomas Applebee, *With a Desire to Help You* by Lauren H. Messersmith, and *When Death Comes into Your Home* prepared by the Quincy-Adams County Ministers' Association in Quincy, Illinois. Of course we must remember that many such customary practices are subject to local variations. Among these practices I shall discuss floral displays, the way the body is displayed, the custom of viewing the remains, the expenditures for the casket and funeral, and the use of the obituary.

Floral Tributes

Floral displays have become a part of virtually all funerals in our time. It would be very difficult to trace the origin of this practice. It is undoubtedly an attempt to beautify an otherwise dismal event. The beautiful lilies and roses and carnations in some way soften the harshness of the bare casket and the severity of some church interiors. Flowers are also sent as tokens of remembrance and sympathy from friends of the bereaved. They are symbols of the sharing of the burden of grief.

So we see that there are negative and positive psychological values in the floral displays at funerals. In one way they are an effort to deny the reality of death by beautifying it. In another they are a demonstration of the solidarity of the community of friends in the sharing of sorrow and loss.

There is an economic factor which also must be taken into consideration. The floral pieces at many funerals represent expenditures of hundreds of dollars. This becomes especially tragic in situations where the bereaved family is in financial need. The dollars which are invested in flowers that wither and wilt in a few hours could be put to much more permanent use in assisting the family to meet its financial obligations or in some more lasting form of a memorial gift.

These facts have caused many churches and pastors to oppose the practice of elaborate floral tributes to the deceased. Some of this opposition has been justified, and some has been based upon fallacious reasoning. Some ministers have suggested that the only real comfort comes from the love of God, not from the sympathetic gestures of relatives and friends. Human sympathy, they say, is not enough. But does this not ignore the important fact, which is consistent with Christian doctrine, that the love of God can be mediated through human expressions of sympathy and love?

A much sounder approach for the reformation of this custom offers another channel for the expression of sympathy and understanding through gifts to the family, the church, or other worthy organizations as memorials. In this way the positive value of expressions of sympathy and the sharing of the feeling of loss is preserved, while the economic wastefulness and the efforts to disguise the reality of death are avoided.

The Casket and Burial Vault

Another problem which is involved in funeral practices is the type of casket and vault which is used. Often bereaved families are moved by various pressures to purchase very expensive coffins and burial vaults and other costly funeral services. It may be the result of high-pressure salesmanship on the part of an unscrupulous mortician, although this is probably not as common as imagined. It may be a matter of social pressure, wanting to "keep up with the Joneses" or fearing that an inexpensive casket may indicate a lack of love or respect for the deceased in the eyes of the community. It may be the result of feelings of guilt, wanting to make a last gesture of recompense for some real or imagined wrong which the bereaved has committed against the deceased. All three of these motivations merit consideration.

High pressuring by an avaricious undertaker is a despicable practice. The bereaved family is under terrific tension, unable to make reasonable decisions, subject to sentimental appeals. In such a condition the family is easily led to overreach itself financially or to purchase professional services which are wholly unnecessary. The church has the right and obligation to oppose such practices by some unscrupulous morticians.

Social pressure is probably the most potent factor in the selection of caskets and other burial services. Our major social stratification is based on economic standing. There is a very potent desire to emulate those in our own class or the class above. This desire sometimes works to the surface in the funeral. There is an important social connotation to having a fine casket and burial vault. A person in the bronze-casket class can hardly drop to the pine-box and mohair class without losing status. The converse is also true— a family may gain in stature by rising from the mohair to the bronze class. Such a desire to maintain or achieve status by doing what others do indicates an extreme dependency and sense of inferiority, which are symptomatic of a lack of personal integrity. This point is self-evident. But what we so often forget is that by depriving people of an outlet for gaining status without providing them a compensating means for achieving selfhood, we do them a disservice. So if the church crusades against expensive caskets, and so on, without recognizing that this is a meaningful way in which some people seek a place in life and without providing another and less superficial way of achieving integrity, it is contributing to spiritual poverty rather than enrichment.

Social pressure also exerts itself by leading people to believe that a beautiful and expensive coffin is a sign of respect and love. Once again we have a symptom of our sensate culture, which decrees that even the deepest feelings of life are determined and measured by material possessions. The church does not accept this premise. But, once again, it cannot resist the custom without providing a more adequate understanding and interpretation of the ways in which love can be expressed.

Purchase of expensive burial accoutrements may have a psychological meaning also. A costly casket may be more than a last gesture of affection for the deceased. It may be a means of seeking relief from a sense of guilt. This fact must not be considered lightly. In spite of all the economic, social, and religious objections to the heavy outlay of money in the funeral, we must recognize that it may be an available outlet for a sense of guilt which, if not released, could bring serious consequences. This does not mean that the pastor encourages such practices, but at least he should be aware of the dynamics of the situation and attempt to understand them. The pastor, if he is aware of such possibilities, if he makes his counsel available to the bereaved even before the funeral, may be able to help the mourners express feelings of guilt and begin to work through them. Then the sense of guilt can be handled in a more therapeutic and less costly way.

There is one other reason for the purchase of expensive and elaborate caskets and vaults. This is the most effective sales point of this equipment: it will preserve the body indefinitely. Not only are the caskets beautiful and stately; they are also self-sealing. Vaults are made of enduring steel or cement and are designed to keep out water and air. One can easily understand the appeal of such advertising: the body which has been loved for many years should be cared for and preserved. From an aesthetic standpoint this may be correct. However, from the point of view of the psychodynamics of grief reactions, this is not helpful. Once again we return to the idea of finality. Burial in a sense typifies the completion of the human element of existence. But if the body is preserved for years and years, even though in the grave, there is still a sense of the presence of the deceased. We think of presence largely in terms of the physical body. So long as this body exists, there is a very subtle and yet meaningful sense of presence. Thus anything which suggests the postponement of the deterioration of the body strengthens the bond of physical presence and the relationship for which it stands, the bond which must be broken if mourning is to be therapeutic.

Although I have no wish to engage in a debate about the relative merits or disadvantages of cremation, I should state that from a psychological viewpoint, which I have just been discussing, cremation is desirable. It most certainly carries with it the idea of finality by demonstrating the immediate disintegration of the body. However, one condition must be added. The whole value of cremation is lost if the ashes of the deceased are not placed in a cemetery or columbarium. The whole therapy of mourning would be endangered if, as some few people do, the ashes were kept in the home of the mourners.

The Display of the Body

The importance of the casket is associated with another of our funeral customs, the display of the body. William F. Rogers gives us a very good outline of the psychological value of the display of the body before the funeral.

Where the body is taken out of the home or hospital and is never seen again, the fact of death may not appear as real to the bereaved, and it is important for them to be confronted with this fact. In addition, the presence of the body tends to stimulate the sympathetic interest of friends, and to make it easier for the bereaved to tell his story over and over again. It may aid in the eventual emancipation of the bereaved person from the deceased, and even to release a sense of guilt.[1]

Having the body prepared for display while lying in state before the funeral often is the source of considerable expense. The casket must be somewhat elaborately furnished with a lining and cushions.

[1] "Funerals in the Light of Our Undertanding of Grief and Bereavement," summarized Report of Joint Session of May 5, 1950, Dept. of Pastoral Services, Commission on Religion and Health, Federal Council of Churches.

The body must be dressed, often with clothing purchased especially for burial. Sometimes extensive cosmetic work is required in addition to the regular embalming process. For these reasons there is a reaction against the display of the body.

Yet there are some values connected with this practice. Sometimes it is helpful in relieving painful memories of a lingering illness or a terrifying accident. One man, whose wife had suffered severe convulsions during the last week of her life, spoke of the comfort which he received by seeing her in repose. The bereavement of Mrs. Lewis, the mother whose little daughter had been killed tragically, referred to in an earlier chapter, was also affected by this part of the funeral custom. A portion of the conversation which took place in one of the calls following the funeral indicates this fact:

Mrs. Lewis: You know, I never thought it would mean so much, but the way the undertaker fixed up Linda's body helped me so much. He did a beautiful job. I didn't think the casket could be opened because she was so bruised and cut. Well, you saw her. But he made her just as beautiful as she always was. He even had her hair fixed the way she always wore it. His mother, who does the hairdressing, said that she used to wear her hair that way when she was a little girl, so she knew just how to do it. When she was in the oxygen tent, her hair was so matted with dirt and burrs and was so much in the way that I was going to cut it off. I'm so glad I didn't. She looked so natural.

Pastor: And seeing her helped you to think of her as she was before the accident.

Mrs. Lewis: I don't think I'll ever be able to get that picture of her poor, hurt little body out of my mind, but it did help to see her for the last time like she always looked.

Pastor: You have to live with both pictures (*stated understandingly, not as exhortation*).

In other cases where death was peaceful, the same thing would be true: it assists the process of remembering the deceased. These memories are usually focused upon a mental image of the deceased. This is a very painful experience because it is a reminder of the harsh fact that the deceased is gone. However, we must not lose sight of the fact that this pain is a necessary part of grief, not for the sake of the pain itself, but for the therapy which comes by it.

Ernest Schachtel informs us that:

Memory as a function of the living personality can be understood only as a capacity for the organization and reconstruction of past experiences and impressions in the service of present needs, fears, and interests. . . . Man perceives and remembers not as a camera reproduces on the film the objects before its lens; the scope and quality of his perceptions and experiences as well as of their reproduction by memory are determined by his individual needs, fear, and interests.[2]

This offers an explanation for the extreme preoccupation of the bereaved with the mental image of the deceased. It is one way in which his need for the deceased is manifested. But it is also true that a downward spiral is set in motion. As his memories fulfill their function, the needs of the individual for the deceased decrease; and as the need diminishes, the memories become less frequent and painful. This is another way of describing the therapy which is accomplished, becoming able to live with the memories of the deceased.

The point which I have been attempting to make is that the display of the body of the deceased has some positive value in that it both demonstrates the end of struggle in repose and aids the process of recalling memories of the deceased.

I have deliberately distinguished between the subject of the display of the body and the matter of viewing the body at the conclusion of the funeral. It is this latter situation which has drawn the fire of many churches and pastors. Some of the reasons (not altogether valid when judged by the criteria set forth here) which have been advanced for opposing it are: it barbarically draws attention to the body rather than the spirit; it is a gruesome practice for those who do not care to look upon the dead; it is an ordeal for the family to sit and watch the silent procession around the bier; it is a real opportunity for the satisfaction of curiosity; it unduly prolongs the service. It must be admitted that this part

[2] On Memory and Childhood Amnesia," A Study of Interpersonal Relations, ed. Patrick Mullahy (New York: Hermitage Press, Inc., 1949) p. 8.

of the funeral customs has become a moment of bad taste and inappropriateness. To insist upon its continuance would almost appear sadistic. Yet any pastor who has tried to reform this practice in his parish immediately encounters resistance. Why is this? Does it mean that people are innately resistant to change, or does it mean that they feel that there is some value in the practice for the mourners?

One value which we can easily detect has already been mentioned in the motives for the selection of expensive caskets, and so on. There is very little point in paying for elaborate coffins and expert preparation of the corpse if there is going to be no opportunity for everyone to see it. The crassness of such a value assures its expendability.

Another value which people find in this practice is an opportunity to demonstrate the solidarity of the community in this crisis situation. The procession to the casket is a way of witnessing to the mutual sympathy of the congregation for the bereaved. As Rogers pointed out, it is also a stimulus for the expression of sympathy to the mourners. There is some positive value in these.

The problem then becomes: How can we preserve the positive values while disposing of the objectionable practice? One solution which is receiving rather wide acceptance is to have the body lie in state before the service for everyone to see either in the days preceding the funeral or before the service begins. The casket is then closed for the service. If the family wishes to take leave of the body before going to the cemetery, the casket may be opened for them privately after the congregation has left the church. This accounts for all the objections except the one which states that the viewing of the body places undue emphasis upon the material rather than the spiritual.

This is truly a problem which is found in every part of the funeral ritual and practices. The funeral has been accused of becoming materialistic. This is based upon the false assumption that religion is concerned only with the spirit and not with the material. Although this statement is often made, its implications are not fully carried out. If religion were purely a matter of the spirit, it would be but one short step into antinomianism. Human conduct would have very little place in the concern of religion. Naturally this is not true. In practice we recognize that a human being is a blend of the material and the spiritual and that these two factors interact. There is a physical element in our religion as well as a spiritual dimension. Now it is true that when death occurs, the unity of body and spirit is in a sense dissolved. But let us ask ourselves if the ordinary mind, especially under the traumatic experience of bereavement, is open to a ready understanding of this distinction. Although we recognize that a man is more than his body, for years in our relationships with that man we have known him and lived with him as he existed in his body. We have not known him apart from his body, even though we recognized that he was more than his physical body. We have known the individual as a whole, a totality; the body has been part of our perception and conception of that individual. When he dies, it is not a simple process for those who have lived in association with this combination of body and spirit to forget immediately all about the body which has represented for them a person whom they have loved. Just as we see mourning as a process which lasts more than several days, we must recognize that the true understanding of the nature of man applied to a deceased loved one does not occur in a moment, in the twinkling of an eye. Can we not see in the funeral an opportunity, as John Wesley stated, "to pay proper respect to what was once a temple of the Holy Ghost"?

In order to become less materialistic, some pastors have proposed discontinuing the practice of funerals in favor of memorial services. The body is buried shortly after death, and a service of memorial for the family and friends is held at a convenient time. Von Ogden Vogt has written a critique of memorial services in which he offers the following objections:

1. A memorial recital of virtues tends to secularity as compared with the thanksgivings, the realizations and the commitments of the burial office. . . .
2. The memorial service fosters human distinctions rather than human equality and solidarity. . . . The memorial service by its very nature takes

account of achievement and distinction and status; the burial office is the same for rich and poor, simple and gifted, king and commoner. . . .

3. The memorial service does not take a proper account of the body. The human person as humanly known is a mysterious compound of body and mind. The true man is not his body, yet cannot exist or function on the earth apart from the body. We rejoice not only in the spiritual life and achievement of our friends but also in their bodily presence. When death closes the eyes and stills the tongue, it is hard for those of long accustomed association instantly to abandon all feeling for the physical habiliments of a loved presence.[3]

These objections imply that the soundest way of removing the objectionable parts of the funeral service is not the discarding of the funeral but the recognition of its personal function as the basis for its reconstruction.

The Obituary

One other feature of the funeral service should be included in this evaluation—the obituary. Reacting to the abuses of the obituary by allowing it to decline into an occasion for flowery oratory and unctuous eulogy, many pastors have discontinued the reading of the obituary. It is also reasoned that it is quite super-fluous to the ritual because the family already knows the pertinent details about the life of the deceased, and friends who were close enough to him in life to make the effort to attend his funeral are also familiar with these details. While all this is true, there is some value in the practice. By recounting the important moments of the deceased's life without eulogy, elaboration, or editorial comment, it is possible to stimulate the memories of the mourners as they relive some of these events. The very fact that some pastors complain that they have omitted the obituary because it caused the family to weep, coupled with Lindemann's statement that thoughts of the deceased brought an onset of the grief syndrome, indicates that this function is fulfilled. Once again I must insist that this is not a sadistic desire to make the funeral hard for people. Rather it is a desire to relieve pain in the long view of mourning even

[3] "We Commit This Body," *The Christian Century*, Mar. 21, 1945, pp. 362-63. Copyrighted by *The Christian Century* and used by permission.

though it may necessitate painful experiences in the present. It has the additional therapeutic value of giving the sanction of religion to the process of remembering, instead of giving people the impression that they are being true to their faith if they push all memory of the deceased from their minds.

Extreme caution must be used in attempts to redirect customs and practices. By becoming a social bull in a china shop, the pastor may break all rapport which he has with his people. If he proceeds solely on the basis of his own predilections and preferences, he is not truly shepherding his people. The key to redirection appears to be in the understanding of the personal needs of the people. If he applies himself to understanding the mourners, recognizing their needs, his efforts to amend the funeral will be in their best interests. It will strengthen rapport and increase the possibilities for future helpfulness in the serious work of grief.

CHAPTER SEVEN

EVALUATING THE FUNERAL SERVICE

ONE PURPOSE of this book is to formulate and expound
a new way of looking at the funeral, through the needs of the
mourners. The establishment of criteria has enabled us to evaluate
the personal function of the funeral in a general way.

The Self-critical Work of the Pastor

However, a corollary purpose of this study of the funeral is to
encourage ministers to evaluate each funeral which they conduct,
to study its effect upon the mourners, to assess the way in which
needs have been met, to determine the validity of funeral services
and practices which they use. If pastors will take the trouble to
evaluate their funerals much more critically, they will be able to
avoid some of the detrimental practices which have been followed
in the name of Christian comfort.

Indeed the pastor should look upon this process of evaluation as
essential to his ministry, for one of the things which aligns the
ministry with the professions is this self-critical, evaluative function. A pastor is much more than a workman who performs the
tasks which he has been taught to do. He is concerned with how
he does his work and is constantly searching for ways in which
his function can be performed more effectively. In order to accomplish this end, he must continually subject his work to critical
evaluation. He must examine his motivation, his method of operation, and the results of his work. He must study the effects of his
work both upon himself and upon the people to whom he ministers.

But evaluation is not enough. To be true to professional standards, it must be accompanied by communication. The findings of
the evaluative process must be made available to other members of

124

the profession. The minister received his training on both the theoretical and the operational levels from a great reservoir of professional knowledge. Through his experience he alters and augments this knowledge with his own unique contributions. However, the process is truncated unless he returns his personal contribution to the reservoir by means of conversations with fellow pastors, discussions in ministerial groups, and the printed page.

Among the pastoral function which require such criticism, evaluation, and communication of findings is the funeral.

Every minister will go about the work of criticizing his funerals in his own way. It would be impossible and foolish to suggest that a standardized check list could be established to assist in this task. It would seem far more advisable to provide a broad outline in which this task could be carried out.

For this purpose a mourning situation and funeral service which come close to the common experience of the average minister will be presented and criticized. The plan of operation is this: as the specific service is being described, I shall interpolate comments indicating why certain elements were used, why other portions might better not have been used. I shall attempt to indicate the strength and weakness of this service. Then following the exposition of the funeral, I shall examine three broad evaluative approaches to demonstrate possible techniques for critical evaluation.

In reading the account of this funeral one should bear in mind the following questions: How does the funeral view death? How does it picture God? What view does it hold of mourning? How does it view the mourners? How can a proper interpretaton of the Christian understanding of death and mourning provide a delineation of some of the more important aspects of the funeral?

This particular situation was selected because it is relatively uncomplicated by guilt and hostility. The service which is described is not intended to be an example of excellence. It is far from that. It is really only a bit of raw material which serves to illustrate the way in which evaluation can be made.

The Situation

Mr. and Mrs. Frye were active members of a midwestern church. They had three children, ranging in age from seventeen to eight years old. Mrs. Frye underwent surgery for an abdominal tumor which proved to be malignant. She lingered for several weeks in great pain and then died. Her death, coming as it did in the prime of life, was a great shock to her family. Although they knew for some days that she could not live, the loss had terrific impact.

Because there were many close relatives living in the same community, many people came to the aid of the motherless family. While this demonstration of family solidarity helped to relieve some of the practical problems accompanying Mrs. Frye's death, it only made the loss seem more apparent. The presence of aunts and uncles, who had often visited in the Frye home, recalled memories of happier days spent in the family circle.

The pastor had called regularly in the home and the hospital during Mrs. Frye's illness. Rapport with all members of the family was very good. During these visits they always requested prayers for Mrs. Frye's recovery, and later for the release from suffering.

As soon as it was learned that Mrs. Frye had died, the minister went to the family home. The members of the family did very little weeping during the call. Funeral arrangements were discussed only very briefly. After the pastor had offered prayer, he asked a few questions which allowed Mr. Frye and the children to speak of the mother. They spoke without reluctance of her last hours in the hospital, seeming somewhat relieved that her suffering was over. The chief difficulty which was apparent at that time was the interpretation of Mother's death to the eight-year-old daughter. The pastor attempted to make some explanation of death in terms of her going to live with God, without in any way implying that it was the wish of God for a mother to leave her family.

The Funeral

The funeral was held in the church with many friends and relatives attending. The following service was led by the pastor:

The Scripture Readings

In the name of the Father, and of the Son, and of the Holy Spirit. Amen. In times of great trouble we seek help in the Word of God.

Lord, thou hast been our dwelling place in all generations. Before the mountains were brought forth, or ever thou hadst formed the earth and the world, even from everlasting to everlasting, thou art God. Thou turnest man to destruction; and sayest, Return, ye children of men. [*The implication of the preceding sentence is that God willfully brings sorrow and tragedy upon men. It may cause the mourners difficulty in seeking the help of God in their plight.*] For a thousand years in thy sight are but as yesterday when it is past, and as a watch in the night. Thou carriest them away as with a flood; they are as a sleep: in the morning they are like grass which groweth up. In the morning it flourisheth, and groweth up; in the evening it is cut down, and withereth. . . . [*This verse implies that the death of an individual is brought about by the intention and the will of God.*] . . . O satisfy us early with thy mercy; that we may rejoice and be glad all our days. Make us glad according to the days wherein thou hast afflicted us, and the years wherein we have seen evil. [*If this verse were accepted uncritically and without a mature perspective, it would undoubtedly foster ambivalent feelings toward God. The picture of God which is presented here and in the verses commented upon above presents God not as a loving Father but as an arbitrary monarch. While the verity of this passage is not questioned when properly interpreted, it is easy to see how the mere reading of these words might create a detrimental confusion in the minds of the mourner.*] Let thy work appear unto thy servants, and thy glory unto their children. And let the beauty of the Lord our God be upon us: and establish thou the work of our hands upon us; yea, the work of our hands establish thou it.

Who can find a virtuous woman? for her price is far above rubies. [*The selection of this passage from the book of Proverbs was an effective means of encouraging the mourners to carry on with the painful but necessary task of recalling memories of the deceased.*] The heart of her husband doth safely trust in her, so that he shall have no need of spoil. She will do him good and not evil all the days of her life. She seeketh wool, and flax, and worketh willingly with her hands. She is like the merchants' ships; she bringeth her food from afar. She riseth also while it is yet night, and giveth meat to her household, and a portion to her maidens. She considereth a field, and buyeth it; with the fruit of her hands she planteth a vineyard. She girdeth her loins with strength, and strengthenth her arms. She perceiveth that her merchandise is good: her candle goeth not out by night. She layeth her hands to the spindle, and her hands hold the distaff. She stretcheth out her hand to the poor; yea, she reacheth forth her hands to the needy. She is not afraid of the snow for her household: for all her household are clothed in scarlet. She maketh herself coverings of tapestry; her clothing is silk and purple. Her husband is known in the gates, when he sitteth among the elders of the land. She maketh fine linen, and selleth it; and delivereth girdles unto the merchant. Strength and honour are her clothing; and she shall rejoice in time to come. She openeth her mouth with wisdom; and in her tongue is the law of kindness. She looketh well to the ways of her household, and eateth not the bread of idleness. Her children arise up, and call her blessed; her husband also, and he praiseth her. Many daughters have done virtuously, but thou excellest them all. Favour is deceitful, and beauty is vain: but a woman that feareth the Lord, she shall be praised. Give her of the fruit of her hands; and let her own works praise her in the gates.

Blessed are they that mourn for they shall be comforted.

Blessed be God, even the Father of our Lord Jesus Christ, the Father of mercies, and the God of all comfort; who comforteth us in all our tribulation.

[*Within this group of scripture readings there are several points worth noting. The first selection, excerpts from Ps. 90, was chosen without much thought, largely because it is among those passages which are often included in the funeral order. Its relevance and meaning in this particular situation were not scrutinized. Thus it could have been, and in this case probably was, of more harm than help. The second selection, Prov. 31, was much more appropriate and meaningful in this situation. Although the imagery and language are from centuries past, the pastor knew the situation well enough to recognize that there were a great many parallels between this ancient picture of the godly woman and Mrs. Frye. The passage might have been abridged somewhat, deleting some of the more irrelevant sections. The New Testament passages seem unduly short and could have been augmented with additional verses, such as selections from the fourteenth chapter of John.*]

The Prayer

Our gracious heavenly Father, bow down thine ear and hear us as we pour out our sorrow before thee. We know that thou art loving and full of compassion, so we draw near to thee for strength and help in our hour of trial. [*Here God is seen as compassionate, accepting the sorrow of his children, a source of help and strength.*]

Although our hearts are heavy with grief, we would thank thee for the blessings which we receive from thy hand. We give thanks for the insight and understanding which we derive from promises to those who mourn. We are most deeply grateful for the light which the knowledge of thy presence sends into the darkness of these days. Alone we could not withstand the weight of the burdens of life. Accompanied by the knowledge of thy love, we find the strength to bear up under our affliction and to walk from the darkness into the day.

We thank thee for the example of love, tenderness, and humility which has been left behind by the mother of this household. [*Here again is aid for the process of recollection.*] May the wisdom and training which she engendered continue to be an inspiration to those who loved her. Bring once again to their minds memories of happier days gone by. [*While the intention of this sentence is good, it could be interpreted as a device for avoiding or escaping the painful or negative experiences of the present.*]

Come with thy blessing, O Father, upon this home, the members of this family. Grant unto them the peace which passeth all understanding, which thou alone canst give. Watch over them, protect them, and guide them in the days and years which are ahead. [*This could include a more explicit promise of the help of God in their time of mourning.*]

Hear our prayers in the name of him who died that we might have life eternal. Amen.

The funeral sermon followed the singing of "Sometime We'll Understand" by a duet.

The Funeral Sermon

In the last chapter of the book of Proverbs there is a description of a godly woman. From the thirtieth verse of that chapter I would like to draw these words: "A woman that feareth the Lord, she shall be praised."

This does not mean that a lengthy eulogy should be given to her life. Rather it indicates that her work is of such importance in the living of godly lives that there is much to be said about it.

The life of a good wife and mother is one of the greatest treasures which man can possess. It is of such value that when that mother passes from our midst, there is left a vast empty and vacant place in our lives. [*This statement accepts the loneliness and loss of the mourners.*] But in a sense there is still something of Mother which remains. The memory of her influence and her love lives on in our lives. [*Here again is aid in the process of recollection. However, a pastor must know the mourners very well to make such a statement. It could easily aggravate guilt feelings or hostility if they are present.*]

It is only natural that there is sadness when a wife and mother takes her departure. The breaking of this close relationship brings with it a deep and painful hurt. The loving deeds, kindly interest, and earnest concern of a mother make up a great part of our lives. When these realities become only memories, one cannot keep the heart from aching and the eyes from brimming with tears. [*This paragraph presents the naturalness and acceptability of mourning.*]

We can be sure that God understands what the loss of a loved one means to us. [*Here it is made clear that God accepts sorrow, that it is not an indication of a deficiency in faith.*] He would not wish us to respond to such a tragic event without any deep feeling. Jesus, when he was called to the grave of his friend Lazarus, wept.

It is not easy to see a life plucked in its full bloom. [*This is a poorly chosen metaphor because it implies that this particular death was caused by some force outside the individual.*] We have great difficulty understanding why such things come to pass. The story is told of a woman who once asked a minister, "Where was God when my son died?"

The pastor replied, "Just where he was when his own Son died."

Perhaps that question has been coming into your minds in these past few days, "Where was God when she died? Why didn't he do something to prevent such loss?" That is the cry of so many suffering people. The answer still is: "God is just where he was when his own Son died. God knows what suffering is too." He knows what you are going through, and he is able to help you. [*This story offers only a minimal contribution to the point which the pastor is making. It would be of greater value if a more explicit exposition were given to the ways in which God is of help to the mourners.*]

One of the most fruitful insights which can come to us as we confront death is that God provides comfort for his people. Even when death breaks our ties with one whom we have loved [*a reminder of finality*], we know that the presence of God is not taken away from us. We are not left desolate and alone. Surrounded by a host of friends and relatives, we are also assured of the nearness of our heavenly Father. His promises to help us in life and death take on new meaning. God will care for your wife and mother in the life beyond, where there is no more pain, nor sorrow, nor trouble. God will care for you and help you through the difficult days which lie ahead. [*Although there is reference here to the help which comes from God and the beloved community, this section would be strengthened by making it apparent that the fellowship of friends and neighbors is a mediator of the love of God. This would bring God's help to the attention of the mourners in more natural and understandable*] terms. *It would more clearly establish the connection between God's help and the process of mourning.*]

It is not easy for our minds to comprehend how sadness and thanksgiving can be experienced at the same time. But even in bereavement we can be conscious of some of the blessings which God has given us. [*This insight is undeniable. However, its presentation would be better if the negative feeling of sorrow would be clearly recognized. Every effort must be made to avoid giving the impression that thanksgiving is substituted for sadness.*] We are reminded that God gives us the blessing and inspiration of memories of the mother who has departed this life. [*While this might appear to be cruel and insensitive, it is a worth-while contribution to the remembering process.*] The guidance, the kindness, the Christian influence, of mother love go with us through the years. Truly this is one of the ways God uses to care for us.

But even more important than that, God gives us the assurance, the hope, of life everlasting. My friends, you face death at a season of the year when Christians everywhere think of death and the resurrection which follows. We are approaching Good Friday with the tragic death on the cross, when the Son of man poured out his life that others might live. We are drawing near to Easter with the stone rolled from the door of the tomb and the exultant song, "O death, where is thy sting? O grave, where is thy victory?" These two things always go together; Good Friday is always followed by Easter. The guarded tomb in Joseph's garden not only held the body of the Master, but with it were interred the hopes and dreams of all his friends. The open sepulcher which was discovered on Easter morn was the birthplace of their hope for resurrection. It was the same grave, but how the meaning had changed! From that time on, Christians have known that death is not the end. While it does draw to a close the relationships we know here, God has promised that those who trust and believe shall not perish. Rather they inherit the gift of life with the Father.

We mourn for the loss of a mother from the family circle, mourn because we are separated from her; but we find strength and endurance in the knowledge that God's presence enables us to face our loss with a multitude of memories of her life and with the assurance that she lives with God. Amen. [*Here, in a few words, the pastor presents a description of the Christian view of mourning.*]

The sermon was followed by the duet "Ivory Palaces" and the benediction. [*The musical selections, which mirrored community custom and the wishes of the family, were helpful only to the extent of the associations which they brought to the minds of the mourners. Both words and music tended toward a sentimental and otherworldly approach to death and mourning.*]

The Committal

Blessed be the God and Father of our Lord Jesus Christ, which according to his abundant mercy hath begotten us again unto a lively hope by the resurrection of Jesus Christ from the dead, to an inheritance incorruptible, and undefiled, and that fadeth not away, reserved in heaven for you, who are kept by the power of God through faith unto salvation ready to be revealed in the last time.

I would not have you to be ignorant, brethren, concerning them which are asleep, that ye sorrow not, even as others which have no hope. [*Without a fuller interpretation this verse can be understood as a mandate not to mourn.*] For if we believe that Jesus died and rose again, even so them also which sleep in Jesus will God bring with him.

The Lord gave, and the Lord hath taken away; blessed be the name of the Lord. [*In such a traumatic experience these words can easily be misunderstood by the mourners. If they either accept this tragedy as the will of God or reproach God for it, they will not be in a position to seek help for mourning from God. In fact mourning then becomes an act of rebellion.*]

Unto the mercy of Almighty God, our heavenly Father, we commend the soul of our sister departed, and commit her body to the ground, earth to earth, ashes to ashes, dust to dust; in sure and certain hope of the resurrection unto eternal life; through Jesus Christ our Lord. Amen.

Let us pray:

Almighty God, whose loving kindness and tender mercies abide with us through all our days, we bow humbly before thee as we lay to rest the earthly remains of thy servant. May her memory live on in us. As we leave this place to go to our homes, may our hearts be filled with thy love, our lives sustained by the hope of eternal life, our spirits quieted by thy peace. In Jesus' name. Amen.

After the benediction a great number of friends came to the bereaved family at the graveside to express their sympathy.

Funeral Practices

There was a very modest number of floral pieces sent by relatives and neighbors of the Frye family. The practice of memorial gifts was not common in this locale. The Fryes expressed their gratitude for the thoughtfulness of their friends, which was demonstrated by the floral tributes and other evidences of shared feeling.

The casket was opened after the service in the narthex of the church. The congregation passed by first, while the family remained in their pews. Then in privacy the family viewed the body. This was the only time that the members of the Frye family showed deep feeling by weeping. The pastor and the undertaker sought to avoid prolongation of this tearfulness by prevailing upon the family to go again to their seats while the casket was closed and placed in the hearse. It would have been far better, since this was not a hysterical outburst, for the pastor to have demonstrated understanding by acknowledging their feelings instead of trying to cut them off.

No vault was used. While this had no bearing on the funeral itself, it did provide the pastor with an opportunity in later contacts with the family to tie together the meaning of burial and its relation to the mourning process.

Evaluation

The earlier statement that it would not be practical to set up a standard pattern for evaluation is substantiated by the fact that evaluation may be approached in at least three different ways. Although they overlap somewhat, each one of them gets down to the basic considerations of what makes the funeral a helpful and beneficial experience.

The Use of the Evaluative Criteria

The first approach consists of an application of the criteria which are proposed in Chapter IV.

The funeral must deal with death realistically. There is nothing in the funeral service which implies an unrealistic view of death. No attempt is made to disguise the fact that death has occurred, nor is the reality of death watered down in euphemism. The whole tone and content of the service represent an effort to clarify and accept the loss which has been sustained by the Frye family. Attention is rightly drawn to the fact that Mrs. Frye has died rather than away from it.

The funeral must present a vision of God which will be of comfort and help to the mourners in their suffering. Herein lies one of the weaknesses of the service conducted for Mrs. Frye's funeral: it does not consistently present God as a source of comfort and help to the mourner. In the sermon it is acknowledged that God understands and accepts sorrowing. This exposition of the permissive nature of the love of God is helpful in allowing the mourners to feel free to express their deep feelings. The knowledge that God understands our feelings is at the very root of therapy. There is also positive value in the statements which are made regarding the care of God for the deceased and the mourners. However, this point could have been made more beneficial by explaining what this divine care involves. There is always the danger that a statement which makes a blanket assertion of God's care can be misdirected into an attitude of resignation under the guise of piety.

On the negative side, there are a number of statements which seem detrimental to the vision of God as a source of comfort and help. The scripture verse which spoke of God afflicting his people, the description of a life "plucked in full bloom," and the passage from Job in the committal service imply that God is the direct cause of the loss which has been suffered by the Frye family. This runs the risk of alienating the mourners from God, conceived as arbitrary and punitive, rather than drawing them to the loving and understanding Father. It should be understood, as was stated in an earlier chapter, that this does not deny the validity of these passages from Scripture; it merely questions the wisdom of using them without ample interpretation of the full meaning.

The funeral must see man as an individual of worth. In a sense this is done. The degree to which the need for integration can be made clear in specific terms will vary with the educational background of the people involved. The simplest way of making this type of individuality evident is by demonstrating that the pastor believes in the importance of ministering to the mourners'

needs. That is done in the Frye funeral. With several exceptions
the service is centered on the mourners. The importance of the
resources of God as aids to personal integration is implicit, although this line of thought could have been developed more fully
and made more apparent in the service. The sermon could indicate
the general line of the therapy of mourning more clearly, yet in
very simple terms. The most important fact to bring out is that
God sees us as individuals of worth and desires that we live lives
which are whole.

*The Christian faith must be seen as a resource rather than a
substitute for mourning.* This matter does not receive clear treatment in the Frye funeral service. The pastor lays the foundation
by presenting an attitude which makes mourning acceptable by
recognizing in the sermon the naturalness of sorrow because of
loss and separation. The sermon also acknowledges that God understands mourning and will be of help to the mourners, but it fails
to be explicit. It could conceivably give the impression that a
firm hold on the Christian faith would obviate mourning. If the
pastor had drawn out more fully what he meant by the help which
God provides, this difficulty could have been avoided. The same
things could be said of the prayer in the funeral service.

*The funeral must recognize and accept deep feelings without
seeking to cover them up with a superficial aestheticism.* On the
whole this is done. The only possible exception is in the musical
selections. The sentimentality of the music and the otherworldly
theme of the poetry of these songs tend to avoid facing reality in
the present in favor of future enlightenment and peace. The choice
of music for the funeral was made by the family without con-
sulting the pastor. This was customary in the community. Under
such circumstances, when the minister does not wish to veto the
choices, he can only hope that the associations which are summoned
forth by this music will be helpful enough to offset the theological
and psychological errors which are propounded.

The funeral must provide a sense of finality. This theme is consistently maintained throughout the funeral. The funeral prayer
and the sermon clearly portray the broken family circle. No doubt

remains that the relationship which has been experienced in the past has now come to an end, and that a new relationship of memory has begun. The act of committal and the prayer at the grave continue this motif.

The funeral service must provide opportunity for beginning the mourning process through remembering the deceased. The use of Prov. 31, with its poetic description of the good wife and mother, is effective in stimulating memories of Mrs. Frye. The reading of this passage had a visible effect upon the mourners. It was apparent that the words were being applied to their own situation. Although this was a somewhat painful experience at the time, it did have therapeutic value in encouraging the remembering process. (However, it must be recognized that a passage such as Prov. 31 would have been a very poor selection if strong guilt feelings had been manifested by the family in the prefuneral call.) The portion of the prayer which expresses gratitude for the exemplary life of Mrs. Frye and the reiteration of this thought in the sermon also assist in the work of remembering.

The funeral must establish a climate for mourning. Recognizing the limitations which have already been noted, we can see several elements in the service which aid in the creation of such a climate. The sermon, with its emphasis on the naturalness of sorrowing and on God's help for facing grief, leads the way. The pastor cannot hope to lay out a full-blown theory of the therapy of mourning in each funeral service. He merely hopes to sow the seeds which will take root and grow in the days and weeks which follow the funeral. The pastoral relationship which he establishes with the mourners following the funeral will have a pronounced effect upon the rate of growth and the yield which the seed brings forth. In this particular funeral service the one element which most seriously weakened the potentialities for a fruitful relationship with the mourners was the picture of God which was given. Postfuneral calls had to confront this problem which existed in the minds of the Frye family and provide a new and different interpretation of God, his love, and the extent of his control over life and death. The attitude which the Fryes had was not one of bitterness, but rather of resignation. A climate for effective mourning was not established until they were helped to a new understanding of the will of God in relation to their lives.

The funeral must be dynamic and sensitive to individual needs. The general theme of this service demonstrates a sensitivity to the needs of the Frye family, but there are several points at which this breaks down. The need for fellowship in sorrow could have been met by participation of the group, the congregation in the service, in the singing of a hymn or the praying of the Lord's Prayer. This is of minor inportance, to be sure; but it would have been a step toward a more sensitive ministry.

A more crucial violation of the needs of the mourners is seen at the moment when the family was standing at the casket at the conclusion of the service. Members of the immediate family burst into tears. Motivated by embarrassment and a misplaced desire to spare the mourners further pain, the pastor and mortician asked them to return to their seats, assuring them that they had done everything possible for Mrs. Frye while she lived and that nothing more could be done. It would have been far better to recognize the depth of the feelings of that moment, acknowledge them, and permit the family a reasonable length of time for this painful leave-taking.

Here very briefly is the type of evaluation which is possible by applying the criteria for improving the personal function of the funeral.

Evaluation by the Assessment of Needs

A second approach to the evaluative task may be made by examining the needs of the mourners and seeking to ascertain how these needs have been met, even though partially, in the funeral service. This can be done by asking a number of questions.

What are the needs of the mourners? No pastor would presume to set himself up as omniscient or infallible, but some skill can be developed which enables the minister to understand the dynamics of the individual situation. Observations made during regular pastoral calls on the family and prefuneral calls with the bereaved provide the major source of such insights. In addition to this some attention should be given to the reactions of the mourners during the service. Observations of those aspects of the service which particularly move the family, for example, can be significant guides for assessing the way that needs are being met. Although this would not have a great effect upon the service itself, it can provide valuable assistance for the continuing ministry to the bereaved after the funeral, as well as being a further check upon the pastor's observations based upon prefuneral contacts.

In the case of the Fryes the minister based a number of assumptions upon his association with the family in the past and upon the feelings which were expressed by members of the family in his prefuneral visit. He knew that the Fryes were not demonstrative people, following a pattern of phlegmatism which was well established in their community. Therefore he did not expect to find a great deal of weeping. Unfortunately the only time there was real weeping in his presence, at the side of the casket, he succeeded in thwarting it, which constituted a rejection rather than an acceptance of the natural reaction to grief.

Other more specific needs which were manifested during the course of the call upon the bereaved family were motivated by loss, loneliness, helplessness, and fear. These feelings were expressed very clearly by Mr. Frye and the older son. They made a number of statements, such as, "How are we going to get along without her?" and, "Things are going to be pretty empty around here now." The pastor took his lead from such remarks, which indicated that the Frye family needed understanding of their loss, acceptance of their loneliness, and recognition of resources of strength, seen in the proper perspective, for relieving their helplessness and fear.

During conversations with the Frye family the pastor did not notice any expressions of resentment or hostility toward anyone. Nor was there any evidence of guilt feelings. The pastor continued to be sensitive to the possibility of such feelings in his dealings with the family after the funeral, but there was no indication of deep-seated ambivalence or guilt.

The next question which is asked in this evaluative approach is: *How well were the needs which were expressed by the mourners met in the funeral service?*

The need for letting out deep feelings which accompany bereavement was only partially met in the funeral. Most of the service maintained a permissive attitude which did not rule out either the feeling or the expression of deep emotion. The naturalness of sorrow was clearly presented. The Fryes were free to express whatever they felt. However, this attitude broke down, as has already been indicated, when it was put to the practical test. The pastor did not allow free expression when the family wept at the closing of the casket. This inconsistency prevented the need for expression from being fulfilled.

The need for understanding the loss which had been suffered was also imperfectly met. On the positive side of the evaluation the funeral worked toward the fulfillment of this need in the realistic and understanding acknowledgment of the pain which was being experienced by the Frye family. The empathetic tone of the funeral, especially the sermon, was good at this point. On the negative side the implications drawn from the view of God which was presented in the funeral were not helpful in the meeting of this need. I have already commented on the way in which the interpretation of death in terms of the will of God deters the mourning process by encouraging either a spirit of resignation to loss or feelings of hostility toward God and guilt because of this enmity. Neither of these attitudes will help the mourner to gain helpful perspective on his loss, while the fact of loss becomes more grievous than ever.

The need for acceptance, that is, understanding, of loneliness was met quite effectively for the Frye family. The funeral service contained a number of elements which aided in the stimulation of memories of the deceased. This implied approval of the remembering process; aided the mourners to understand the meaning of their loneliness, that is, the fact of the broken human relationship; and also provided a means by which the loneliness could be eased. The same thing could be said of that portion of the sermon which recognized the feeling of vacuousness which followed Mrs. Frye's death. The acknowledgment of these feelings is a prior step to dealing with them. Once the mourners feel free to express themselves, to bring to the surface their feelings, the therapy of mourning can begin its work.

The need for recognizing resources of strength to deal with fear and helplessness was met in part. Without the indication of specific portions of the funeral, it is possible to summarize some of the helpful ideas which were given to the mourners. God is identified as the source of strength. The mourners are reminded of God's presence, his love, his understanding of their situation, his gift of new life. This is as it should be. These are essential elements of Christian comfort. The one weakness is the lack of interpretation bearing upon the use of these resources. As the service was conducted, one might receive the impression that it is a one-way relationship, that the mourners passively wait for God to pour the balm of comfort upon them. It lacks a vital and dynamic presentation of faith as an active response to man's understanding of God. The need of the mourners would have been more fully met if they had been led to see more clearly that the resources of God would enable them to engage in the work of mourning, instead of accepting the implication that mourning was obviated by having faith. In a sense this is another way of applying the axiom that faith without works is dead.

By asking the questions: What are the needs of the mourners? and, How are these needs met in the funeral? the pastor can evaluate the effectiveness of the funeral in aiding people to mourn.

Evaluation by Interpretation of Attitudes

A third approach for evaluating the funeral is an adaptation of a technique which Seward Hiltner teaches for the critical evaluation of pastoral counseling. We look at the funeral in terms of three focuses: the mourners, the pastor, and the relationship between the pastor and the parishioner. A combined view of these three factors gives a fairly complete picture of the effectiveness of the funeral.

Focusing upon the mourners involves much of what is done in the two other evaluative approaches. The pastor seeks to ascertain what are the particular problems which the mourners face in this situation, what are their needs, how are they reacting in the grief situation. It is important for the pastor to observe the postfuneral reactions of the mourners as well. Since this book is concerned with the funeral rather than with counseling the bereaved, I might be tempted to omit a consideration of postfuneral reaction. However, the minister can learn a great deal about what was accomplished in the funeral by carefully weighing the reaction of the mourners against the content and technique of the funeral. Such an evaluation will not only point the pathway for further counseling with the bereaved; it will also enable the pastor to correct and improve his funeral ministry in other grief situations.

There is no need to reiterate the discussion of the needs of the Frye family, nor the way in which this particular funeral succeeded or failed in meeting those needs. If this third evaluative approach were used exclusively, this aspect of the needs of the mourners would have to be fully explored at this point.

The postfuneral reaction of the Fryes clearly indicated some of the errors which were made in the funeral. There was some difficulty encountered because of the interpretation of God and his relationship to his children in the funeral. For a time the Fryes accepted their bereavement stoically, resigned to what they supposed to be the will of God, piously and sincerely believing that keeping their faith in God strong would heal the wound. It would be a mistake to assume that this was wholly the result of the funeral, but the funeral did not do enough to shift the previous mind-set of the mourners. Another way in which the postfuneral reaction was affected by the funeral was seen in the stringent emotional control which the Fryes exercised when the pastor called. Once again this was not completely due to the funeral, but it must be admitted that if their pastor had not thwarted their emotional expression after the funeral service, they might have felt free to react as they felt in his presence later on. The pastor would have been thought of as an agent of release rather than one of sublimation.

This leads to the second focal point: the attitude of the pastor.
The minister can learn something about the validity and effectiveness of his funeral ministry by examining his own attitude in the
situation. None of us believes that a pastor is a passive vessel,
making no uniquely personal contribution to his work. The attitudes and temperament of the pastor have as much to do with
the pattern of his work as does his theological position.

For example, in the Frye funeral the minister felt ill at ease
when the family broke down. Not only was he embarrassed; he
also had vague feelings that the success of his work was being
threatened. He had tried to bring a message of comfort and hope.
The emotional reaction of the Fryes was mistakenly understood
by him as a sign that his ministry at this point was ineffectual.
Because he saw this as a threat, he moved to end it by encouraging
the Fryes to compose themselves.

This is but one illustration of the way in which the attitude
of the minister can have an effect upon the funeral. This process
works positively as well as negatively. In this same funeral the
attitude of the minister made him somewhat sensitive to the needs
of the mourners. Although his way of meeting those needs was
far from perfect, the fact remains that he saw them.

If the pastor will critically examine his own motivations, his
own attitudes, additional light will be thrown upon his analysis
and evaluation of the funerals he conducts.

*The third focus deals with the relationship between the pastor
and the bereaved.* While it is recognized that the ministry is not
merely a process of making friends and influencing people, it must
be said that the establishment of rapport is essential to the pastoral
obligation. Does the funeral strengthen or strain rapport? The
answer to that question has a distinct bearing upon the effectiveness of the funeral. Seeing the funeral as a precounseling opportunity makes this point crucial. If the pastor estranges himself or
the church from the family, he places serious obstacles in the pathway of any help which might be given to the mourners.

In the case of the Fryes the pastor both strengthened and weakened rapport. He was understanding at some points, such as his

recognition of the sense of loss and loneliness; but at other points, for example, his failure to appreciate the significance of weeping and his implicit placing of the responsibility for the death of Mrs. Frye on the will of God, he lacked sensitivity. Had it not been for the excellent rapport which existed between the minister and these parishioners before the crisis, the pastoral relationship might have been severely damaged.

In evaluating the funeral this point of view would indicate that those factors which deepen the pastoral relationship are good, while those which breach it are ineffectual.

It was stated earlier in this chapter that no attempt was being made to formulate a standardized check list for evaluating the funeral. For this reason several different approaches have been discussed. The fact that they have overlapped indicates that an evaluation can be made with any or all of them. It remains for the individual pastor to adapt them to his primary concerns, using them as he sees fit to gauge the effectiveness of the personal function of the funeral services which he conducts.

CHAPTER EIGHT

PASTORAL CARE AS A CONTEXT
FOR THE FUNERAL

IF THE FUNERAL is to minister to personal needs, as has been proposed, certain emphases will have to be made in the parish work of the minister. Whenever the pastor is dealing with an individual, his total ministry has an effect upon the relationship. In spite of the modern tendency toward specialization, the whole of the ministerial functions must be consistent and integrated. The ministry which a pastor offers in a funeral cannot be isolated from the many other functions and responsibilities which he has. His funeral service will lack effectiveness if it is out of step with his Sunday sermons, his pastoral visitations, his handling of people in the administrative work of the parish. One of the most apparent evidences supporting this fact is seen in the significant relationship between pastoral care of the bereaved and the funeral which the pastor conducts.

It is not the intention of this chapter to present a fully developed treatment of pastoral care in general, or even pastoral care of the bereaved. This subject has been ably, although briefly, described in such books as R. C. Cabot and R. L. Dicks, *The Art of Ministering to the Sick,* pp. 315-28; Carroll A. Wise, *Pastoral Counseling, Its Theory and Practice,* pp. 206-18; and William Rogers, *Ye Shall Be Comforted,* pp. 33-48. Here pastoral care is being dealt with only as it has bearing upon the funeral, as it forms a context for the funeral.

The ministry to the bereaved is a whole composed of several parts. It is not made up solely of conversations with the mourners, nor is it only the funeral service. These functions of the minister interact; the funeral contributes to pastoral care, and pastoral care makes a contribution to the funeral. Concentrating on the funeral, as has been done here, does not imply that it is superior to all other aspects of the ministry to the bereaved; it only affirms a consistent effort to maintain the focus of this book upon the funeral. Therefore it should be understood that pastoral care is considered as a context for the funeral only for the purposes of this volume. It would be just as correct to see the funeral as a context for studying pastoral care in bereavement.

An understanding of the personal function of the funeral and its therapeutic possibilities necessitates more than a little work with the bereaved before and after the funeral. This whole approach to the funeral presupposes that the minister will be diligent in his pastoral care of the mourners. As the discussion takes up the consideration of prefuneral and postfuneral calls upon the bereaved, it will be apparent that just to make a series of visitations is not enough. What happens during these calls assumes new pertinence.

Prefuneral Calls

Various manuals of pastoral work which have been published through the years have counseled ministers to have a purpose for making their calls. This suggestion is helpful so long as the purpose remains flexible. One can easily see the folly of entering the home of a parishioner with a purpose in mind and then steadfastly holding to that design without any sensitivity to problems or needs which are manifested during the call. But to carry flexibility to the extreme of giving no thought to the purpose of pastoral visitation is equally foolish.

There are numerous purposes which a pastor might have in mind when he calls in the house of mourning: making funeral arrangements, expressing sympathy, establishing rapport, assisting in the acceptance of the mourning process, and evaluating the dynamics of the mourning situation. In all of these the minister has the opportunity to demonstrate and to offer the resources of the Christian faith to the mourners.

Probably the most common aspect of the prefuneral call is the making of plans for the funeral. There has to be some meeting of minds between the mourners and the pastor in arranging all the details of the funeral service. As the undertaking profession assumes more and more of a place in the actual conduct of a funeral, this purpose of the prefuneral call is being minimized. Very often the mortician is either the initiator of most of the funeral plans, or he serves as a mediator, passing on the wishes of the family to the pastor. While we are not justified in objecting to or resenting every service offered by the undertakers, we should recognize that even the making of the arrangements for the funeral services carries with it very real opportunities for improving the personal function of the funeral. These will become more apparent as we explore the other purposes of the prefuneral calls. If the pastor is convinced that opportunities for understanding and therapy exist in the making of funeral arrangements, there is nothing to prevent him from reviewing the details with the mourners, even after the mortician has formulated these plans.

A second common purpose for prefuneral calls is the expression of sympathy to the bereaved. This can be a very meaningful moment in the pastoral relationship. The pastor speaks for himself in offering condolences. He is demonstrating his concern and love for those whose lives are in need of reassurance and support. But he also speaks as a representative of the church, the Christian community, bringing in his words an appreciation of the loss which has been sustained by the friends and neighbors of the deceased and evincing the sympathetic concern of the entire beloved community.

This first expression of sympathy is the beginning of the process of understanding and acceptance which will be carried on in the funeral. Therefore it is extremely important that sympathy be expressed in a way which is consistent with the whole approach to mourning. So many of the clichés which are used in such circumstances afford less help than harm. To say, "I am sorry to hear of your loss, but you must be brave and have faith," or "We know that God always does what is best for us, even though we do not perfectly understand it," will do very little to abet the therapeutic process of mourning. Such statements subtly deny the necessity of mourning, are insensitive to the deep needs of the individual, and rob the bereaved of vital resources for meeting this crisis situation. How much better it would be to say, "We are so very sorry that Mr. Smith has died. I think we can all understand in a small way your loss because we are all going to miss him. If there is anything that I can do to help you through this difficult time, I hope you'll call on me." Here we have in essence a statement which demonstrates empathy, which acknowledges loss, which manifests concern, which opens the door for assistance in the work of mourning. It does nothing to discourage the expression of feelings, nor does it tell the mourner how he ought to feel. Such expressions of sympathy can have a constructive effect on the pastoral care which the minister offers to this bereaved family.

A third purpose of the prefuneral call is the establishment of rapport. While this is a basic function of any pastoral care, it is extremely important in situations of bereavement. Superficially a pastor might consider himself in rapport if he merely felt sad along with the family of the deceased, or if he sympathized with them. In reality more effective rapport would be based upon the pastor's attitudes of receptiveness, acceptance, empathy, and understanding. If the minister demonstrates that he is willing for the mourner to express his feelings, whatever they might be, that he understands and is concerned with the deep needs of the mourner, that he has a mature view of death and bereavement, a bond will be established which will make for helpful pastoral care. If, on the other hand, the minister imposes his own views on grief, if he tries to argue the mourner out of what he is feeling, if he fails to appreciate the situation of the grief-stricken, if he betrays an attitude of detached professionalism, the entire pastoral relationship is placed in jeopardy.

In a great many situations rapport will have been established in the pastoral relationship before death takes place in a home. However, the ministry to the bereaved can either build upon previous rapport or destroy it. The effectiveness of the funeral service and of the whole therapeutic activity of mourning leans heavily upon the relationship which the pastor is able to establish or sustain in the prefuneral calls.

Another purpose of these calls is the rendering of assistance in the mourning process. These contacts not only establish rapport between the pastor and his people; they also provide an opportunity for people to talk about their loss. During these visits the contribution of the pastor to the therapy of mourning is really beginning. The funeral becomes a continuation of the process, because the minister is evincing the same understanding and receptiveness which he has demonstrated in earlier visits.

There are a number of ways in which people can be helped to talk about the loss which they have experienced. For example, when the funeral arrangements are being made, the pastor requires vital information about the deceased for use in the obituary or the parish records. A simple exposition of the important dates and relationships in the life of the deceased very often provides the mourners with a valuable opening to talk about him. They speak of his parents, his marriage, his work, the birth, and perhaps the death, of his children. They mention his church affiliation and social relationships. They discuss his age, the length of his illness, the time at which he died. By asking questions such as, "Were you at the hospital when your father died?" or, "Did he ever rouse from the coma?" the pastor will enable the mourners to begin to think about and talk about the painful memories of those events which transpired at the time of death and shortly before. The astute pastor will realize that this is a difficult and painful experience for the mourners. If he senses any reluctance on the part of the mourners to engage in this activity, he will not press the matter. He will immediately be alert to any other indications of unwillingness to face the reality of death, or to any signs of a desire to escape from this painful experience, or to any manifestations of ambivalence toward the deceased or guilt feelings which might make it extremely difficult to recall or speak of the deceased.

Once again it must be repeated that the purpose of these pre-funeral calls is not to probe for the various feelings which the pastor suspects might be present. The purpose is to enable people to talk, to bring out their feelings voluntarily. The pastor accepts

them and reflects them, enabling the individuals to see themselves and the reasons why they feel as they do.

Another way in which the prefuneral calls can assist the mourning process is in analysis of basic attitudes toward death and
bereavement. This is really a twofold process. In the first place,
the pastor seeks to understand the attitudes of the mourners through
his conversations with them and his observations of their responses
and activities. From what they say and do he will be able to
determine whether they are facing their loss or evading it, whether
they are expressing their real feelings or those which they feel will
be socially acceptable, whether they see the Christian faith as a
resource for mourning or a means of escape from it, and whether
or not they recognize the adjustment which must be made. Secondly, the basic attitudes toward death and bereavement which
are demonstrated by the pastor himself are important for the
effectiveness of the prefuneral calls. This does not mean that he
must argue his position against that of the mourners. But the
evident witness of his mature view of death and the work of
mourning will make a contribution to the pastoral care which is
given, even when he is accepting the attitudes of the mourners.
This is not to say that he will explicitly propose the acceptance
of his views or the adoption of a plan of mourning which he suggests. However, it does mean that he will show in his own attitude
toward this crisis situation that he considers death as a reality
which draws to a close the relationships with the deceased, that
he accepts the loss which has been sustained as a fact, that he
looks upon the Christian faith as a means of meeting and working
through grief, that he recognizes the difficult adjustments which
will now have to be made.

Still another way in which the prefuneral calls aid the work of
mourning is seen in the bringing of the resources of the Christian
faith to the situation. This work must begin at the level of the
faith which the mourners already possess. It is apparent that a
pastor cannot hope to manufacture a mature faith on the spot for
the bereaved, if they are deficient in faith. The prefuneral calls,
as has been said of the funeral, are not the occasion for an effective

presentation of a fully developed exposition of the Christian view of death and resurrection. It must be borne in mind that the pastor is dealing with people who are undergoing a traumatic experience and who are not in the proper frame of mind to engage in detailed intellectual activity at this time. It is far more reasonable to suppose that the meaningfulness of the Christian view of death and resurrection will come to them with greater clarity when they are able to reflect upon their loss after the first shock waves have rolled over them.

In the same way the prefuneral calls are not to be seized upon as opportunities for the pastor to exhort people to have faith. Theologically we recognize that faith is man's response to the grace of God, that there must be a readiness in man before faith will be a reality in his experience. To require of people that they have faith when they feel no readiness for it is to present an impossible course of action, as well as to risk the danger of stimulating guilt feelings because of the inability to have faith under these circumstances. For the person who possesses a mature faith before the crisis strikes, the issue is not so acute. But even then the pastor will do well not to get too far ahead of the parishioner in his expectations that this faith will be brought to bear upon bereavement until the mourner has had the opportunity to give full expression to his feelings.

How, then, can the resources of the Christian faith be presented apart from exposition or exhortation? One means of presentation is through the experience of Christian fellowship. The concern of the pastor and other members of the community of Christians is evidence of the love of God mediated through human love. Whether or not the person goes to the extent of following out this reasoning, the love of God is still ministering to him in his time of need. The sharing of his sorrow is a direct outgrowth of the Christian faith—"the tie that binds our hearts in Christian love."

Another way in which the resources of the faith are presented is in the freedom with which the mourner is allowed to express himself. The accepting and permissive attitude of the pastor in allowing the mourner to express his weakness, his doubt, his bitterness, his sorrow, his needs, should be seen as representative of the accepting and forgiving nature of God. That which clarifies the nature of God contributes to the formulation and acceptance of faith.

The resources of the Christian faith are also presented in the scripture readings and prayers of the pastor in the prefuneral calls. The same principles which were elaborated in the discussion of the funeral service, Chapter V, would pertain in the selection of scripture passages and the content of prayers. Passages from the Bible such as Ps. 27, Ps. 46, and the New Testament account of Jesus at the tomb of Lazarus in John 11 are typical of selections which offer excellent possibilities for interpreting the meaning of death and mourning. Prayers which commend the spirit of the deceased to God, which express gratitude for living memories of the departed, which seek the help of God for the work of mourning, will be helpful in both a devotional and a didactic sense. However, we must keep in mind the unique situation involved, using only those thoughts which will be helpful and not harmful to the particular mourners to which the pastor is ministering.

An additional means of assistance in the mourning process comes from the contribution which is made by the faith of the pastor, his vital conviction that God is the loving Father who abides with his children in life and in death. There is a contagious nature to faith in the God of mercy who understands the needs of his children and who accepts them in spite of their weakness. The underlying confidence with which the pastor faces this crisis situation need not necessarily come through a verbalization of his faith if it is apparent that this faith forms the basis for his operating procedures.

These various aspects of pastoral care in the prefuneral calls which aid the bereaved to accept and undertake the mourning process form a basis upon which the funeral service can continue this ministry to the grief-stricken.

The last of the five purposes which have been assigned to the prefuneral pastoral care is the evaluation of the dynamics of the particular grief situation. These prefuneral calls have a diagnostic function. By carefully weighing the conversations which take place, the pastor is often able to gain insight into the feelings and motives of the mourners. These observations provide a basis upon which a funeral service that is sensitive to the needs of the bereaved can be constructed.

The minister, in addition to noting the degree of emotional reaction, should be aware of the feelings which the mourners express, either explicitly or implicitly. Such feelings might be considered in three categories: the feelings of the mourner toward himself, toward the deceased, and toward others.

First, what are the feelings which the mourner expresses toward himself? These may be positive feelings, which indicate progress toward a healthy adjustment. He may say, "Pastor, this has been a hard blow for me. But I know that even though I did everything I could to keep Mother with me, I'm just going to have to learn to go it alone." Such a statement does not necessarily guarantee adjustment, but it is an indication of the mourner's thoughts and feelings about himself. He is saddened and torn, but he has resolved to assimilate the experience and rise above it.

Contrast this with the negative feelings toward the self manifested in remarks such as these: "I wish I'd realized how serious this was. I would have taken Mother to a doctor sooner." Or a mourner might say, "If only we had made things a little bit easier for Dad, he might not have had this heart attack. We didn't know his heart was weak." Such statements give the pastor insight into the possibility of guilt feelings. He would suspect the existence of much deeper guilt if the mourner were to say, "I'm the one who should be dead. It is my fault that the accident happened. I wish I were dead."

The pastor should also be sensitive to expressions of utter confusion or a sense of futility. "What's the use of going on living? There's nothing left for me now." Remarks such as these are certainly not to be accepted as sole evidence of states of depression or guilt feelings. They have to be seen in the wider context of the contacts with the parishioner. They are like weather vanes, which indicate the direction of the mourner's current of thought and feeling, but do not by themselves measure the intensity of the wind.

Secondly, the astute pastor will observe the feelings which the mourners express toward the deceased. These, too, can be either positive or negative. We would classify as positive such feelings which denote love, gratitude, devotion, respect, and so on. A minister often hears, "John was a wonderful man. He was the kindest, most thoughtful person." Recognizing that there is a strong possibility of idealization, weighing such statements against his own knowledge of the facts, the minister nevertheless sees the apparent ease of remembrance which gives promise of the successful beginning of therapy.

Sometimes there are negative feelings manifested: "You know, Pastor, that George never did come to church. He was a good-enough man, but I just had to fight with him to let the children come to Sunday school." Or a mourner might remark: "I told him to take things more slowly, but he just wouldn't listen to me. He never would do what I told him to do." There is not sufficient grounds for assuming that a deep-seated hostility is present here, but the acceptance of such negative feelings would free the mourner to further expression and would give the pastor valuable insight into both the domestic situation and the dynamics of the mourner. Strong negative feelings against the deceased are rarely evidenced because of the taboo against speaking ill of the dead. They are much more likely to come out in terms of the third type of observation.

The minister will note carefully feelings which are expressed by the mourner toward other people, such as relatives, neighbors, the attending physician, the pastor, and the church. Positive feelings of gratitude for assistance in crisis, for expressions of sympathy, point to an understanding of the solidarity of the fellowship. Often mourners say, "Folks have just been wonderful to us. It really helps to know that everyone cares so much."

On the other hand, a minister might hear, "What good did all the praying do? Why didn't God save her? I don't think I can ever have faith again." Or a mourner will say, "If Dr. X were any good, she'd still be here. He just didn't know what was wrong with her until it was too late. Oh, why didn't we go to a better doctor?" Such feelings, as has been stated in an earlier chapter, may give vent to hostility, which is the outgrowth of the sense of frustration which often accompanies death. They may be genuine hostility against the person mentioned, or they may be a projection of hostility which is really felt against the deceased but is expressed against a third person. In any case they are negative feelings which should be recognized by the pastoral counselor as a significant factor to be dealt with in the work of mourning.

Since this volume is not concerned with pastoral counseling per se, even in the grief situation, the explicit treatment of counseling technique has been omitted. However, the acceptance of negative feelings is so important for the establishment of the therapy of the mourning process that there is justification for touching very briefly upon the matter of technique.

Take, for example, the statement made above, "What good did all the praying do? Why didn't God save her? I don't think I can ever have faith again." How will the pastor respond? One approach would be to take the edge off such a statement by countering it with something of a positive nature. The pastor answers, "Now, Bob, you know you don't mean that. Things will seem brighter to you after the first shock is past. After all, you remember how you've been taught that God answers prayers in different ways. This will all work out for the best," and so on. This is nonacceptance. For all the good intentions of the pastor, he has laid the foundation for a barrier between himself and Bob which will cool the warmth of the pastoral relationship and create a defensive spirit in the parishioner which will negate possible good that might be done in his counseling and the funeral service. Instead of getting out the gnawing negative feelings, Bob will shove them down when he is in the presence of his pastor, because he knows that to discuss them will bring on a sermon, which indicates that the minister is working against him instead of with him.

The other approach would be to recognize and accept the negative feeling as such. The pastor answers, "A blow like you've had makes you feel pretty bitter, as though the things you've trusted in have let you down." He does not necessarily agree with Bob, but he understands and accepts what the parishioner is feeling without passing judgment on the weakness of his faith or attempting to give him a shot of spiritual vitamins. Bob thinks, "Here is a man who understands what I am feeling. I can talk to him about the things that are bothering me without getting argument or pep talk." And the doorway to a helpful funeral and counseling relationship is opened.

It is true that there would be grave danger of doing real damage if the minister were to make snap judgments about the psychic ills of his people or attempt to engage in a type of primitive psychoanalysis with them. He could do very real harm to people if, for example, he went about probing for guilt feelings or attempting to do depth therapy.

There is a certain protection against this in the type of pastoral counseling which is variously called client-centered, reflective, or eductive. It is against the background of this sort of counseling that this book is written. If a pastor counsels in this fashion, he merely seeks to understand the feelings which are expressed by the parishioner. He accepts those feelings and reflects them so that the inner resources of the parishioner may work through them. His evaluation of the dynamic forces operative within the parishioner is made not to enable him, the pastor, to prescribe treatment but to enable him better to understand and accept the person with whom he deals.

In evaluating forces within the grief reaction the pastor is not engaged in diagnosis for the purpose of being able to treat the bereaved by dispensing the proper advice. When he realizes that there are feelings of guilt present, he does not reach for his guilt pills. When he detects ambivalence, he does not spoon out the hostility tonic. He merely takes these feelings into account in his ministry to the bereaved in order to do nothing which will accentuate them and in order to make it apparent that the resources of

Christianity enable a man to grow beyond them. When he proposes the availability of such resources, he always does so in a way which leaves the parishioner free to accept or reject them. Under no circumstances will he force his evaluation or his therapy upon the parishioner. He will recognize that preservation of the freedom and responsibility of the mourner is a vital part of the therapy.

There is always the danger of reassurance which comes too easily. To approach the mourners with the words, "You'll get over it," or with that attitude, will render no assistance to them. There is not comfort in a superficial, "silver-lining" optimism. Real help comes from an attitude of quiet confidence, faith, and hope.

The expression of any positive or negative feelings by the mourners should have an influence upon the funeral service which the pastor prepares to meet their needs. The prefuneral pastoral work of the minister takes on great significance when the personal approach to the funeral is made.

In view of the several purposes of the prefuneral calls it is apparent that the pastoral care of the bereaved before the funeral cannot be given adequately in one brief call. If the pastor is to establish rapport, assist in the acceptance of the mourning process, and understand the dynamics of the particular grief reaction, he will have to speak with the family at some length. Two brief visits would probably be much more helpful than one extended call. It must be recognized that to spend this much time with the family will in some cases be difficult or impossible because of the busyness of the family in these days or, as in the case of the South, where burial is made on the day following the death. However, the pastor will do well to strive for the ideal.

One of the reasons for calling in the house of mourning is to give evidence of the concern of the Christian community. Thus it would seem desirable for the minister to make his first call as soon as possible after receiving notification that death has occurred. Most of the brochures which are being published by ministerial groups to reform community funeral practices contain some reference to encourage mourners to call their pastor immediately when a parishioner dies. This is an excellent trend.

All too often the minister is not notified until the first phase of the grief reaction has taken place and the business of arranging the funeral is being considered. Before we go too far in condemning our parishioners for their thoughtlessness or accusing the mortician of assuming too much responsibility, it would be well for us to ask why it is that the pastor is not called earlier. Is it not possibly a commentary upon the type of ministry to the bereaved which has been offered in the past? Perhaps some people want to express their grief in their own way before they face the minister, who represents control, repression, and "faith." It is conceivable that the reluctance of some people to summon their pastor immediately could be overcome by improving the pastoral care which is offered to the bereaved.

Various solutions have been suggested to create a greater readiness on the part of church people to call their minister when death occurs. It has been proposed that the minister must keep in close touch with all families who are undergoing a crisis, thereby developing rapport with them and earning their confidence. It has also been suggested that the pastor has to educate his congregation to the availability of his ministry in any circumstances, so that they will call on him readily whenever they stand in need of his ministration. Another recommendation is that the minister answer the summons of his parishioners promptly and with dispatch, demonstrating that he recognizes the urgency of their need and is concerned with it. These points are all well taken, but we must recognize that the mere fact that a minister calls on the bereaved immediately following the death is not nearly as important as what he does once he gets there.

It is essential that the pastor bear in mind the situation of the mourners shortly after death has occurred. In most cases they will be physically and emotionally exhausted, tense, confused, out of touch with reality. Unless the pastor is understanding and accepting of the things they say and do, he will fail miserably in his first contact with them. His presence during this first period of shock is important both for the concern which it indicates and because of the opportunity which it affords him to observe the dynamics of the mourners before repressive controls and defenses are established.

Another call would then be made after the family has had an opportunity to think about the funeral service. The visit would concern itself with the details of the service. Even here the opportunities for pastoral care are legion. There is some aid for the mourning process in memories of the deceased stimulated by obituary data, discussion of favorite hymns or scripture passages of the deceased. There are diagnostic possibilities in the attitudes toward death and bereavement which are manifested by the mourners as they discuss the funeral plans. One can often see escapist techniques in their incipient stages in this phase of the pastoral care of the bereaved. These are dealt with far more easily at this point than at a later time when they have become consolidated. To reflect the feelings of the mourners which are apparent in the making of the funeral plans will serve to bring these feelings and motivations from the unconscious to the conscious level of their thinking.

Sometimes the pastor is consulted about burial details as well. There are occasions when ministers have felt a responsibility to deter the family from undue extravagance or from bowing to social pressures to meet certain community standards of burial practices. However, in the light of the underlying theory of counseling which forms the basis for this entire discussion of the funeral it is not particularly beneficial for the pastor to be a problem solver, making the necessary decisions for the family or dissuading them from their plans. It is far better for him to reflect the feelings and motivations of the mourners as they make their decisions, with the confidence that a clarification and understanding of the dynamics of the situation will enable the mourners to make decisions which will be beneficial to them. In this way the minister will be fulfilling his pastoral obligation, yet will be respecting the freedom of the mourners by refraining from imposing his opinions upon them. For example, we recognize that often extravagances in funerals are motivated by a sense of guilt for some real or imagined wrong done to the deceased. The pastor, when he recognizes this situation, can do one of two things. He can directly urge the mourners not to make exorbitant expenditures for the funeral, or he can reflect the feelings which are evidenced in the conversation of the mourners in such a way that they will be conscious of why they feel the pressure to have an elaborate burial. The first course of action will do nothing to deal with whatever guilt feelings may be present. The second plan of operation does not necessarily guarantee successful adjustment. The mourners may reject the reflection of the feelings which they have expressed and may continue in their elaborate arrangements. Or they may begin to think things through and with the pressure somewhat relieved modify their arrangements. But in either of the latter two alternatives the door is open to future counseling.

The function of the prefuneral calls goes far beyond the usual conception of this ministry. They cannot be dealt with in the common sympathy-reassurance-arrangement pattern which is so often followed.

There is one other aspect of the prefuneral work which remains to be discussed. Although it comes before the calls mentioned above in the time sequence, it is appended here because it is not a part of every grief situation which the pastor meets. Prefuneral pastoral care in some situations includes the ministry to the dying. Once again I am, for the purposes of this discussion, not concerned with a detailed exposition of the ministry to the dying; I deal with it only as it has an effect upon the ministry of the funeral.

One of the most apparent contributions which the pastoral care of the deceased before his death makes to the funeral is the rapport which has been established with the family. Every pastor who has been in parish work, even if for only a short time, knows the deep bond of fellowship which grows between him and the families to which he has ministered in crisis.

In speaking of this development of rapport, I am presupposing that the minister was present in accordance with the wishes of the family, although not necessarily at their direct invitation. There is no rapport developed in the type of situation which one sometimes encounters where a minister has intruded into a sickroom to do his duty in the saving of souls, has unduly disturbed the patient, or has violated all the standards of good taste and judgment in the name of pastoral ministration. But assuming that the pastor's presence has the approval of the family, the way is opened for a very fruitful relationship on a continuing basis. The prefuneral calls, the funeral itself, the postfuneral pastoral care are made much easier and freer because the mourners feel that here is a man who has been through the ordeal with them and is concerned with their needs. There is an intimacy born in the ministry in crisis situations which is a tremendous boon to all future pastoral relationships.

The pastoral care of the dying also contributes to the funeral ministry through the opportunity which it offers to the pastor for observing the attitudes of the family toward themselves, toward the patient, toward death. The minister can see in advance patterns which will characterize the grief reaction.

How does the family comport itself when death is imminent? Is there panic, bitterness, fearfulness, escape, phlegmatism? Careful observation of such factors will prepare the pastor for dealing with these feelings when they are expressed in later contacts. He will take cognizance of those facts which might indicate that the members of the family are attempting to seal themselves off from the realities of the situation. He will note their desire and ability to adjust to the crisis.

In the same fashion important observations can be made of the way in which the family acts toward the dying person. A simple thing like the effort to keep the patient ignorant of the gravity of his condition, which symbolizes an overprotective attitude, if it is done on the initiative of the family rather than on the counsel of their physician, may be indicative of guilt feelings toward the one who is dying. Overprotectiveness, even apart from these circumstances, is often symptomatic of a deep-lying resentment and the concommitant guilt feelings. On the other hand, if the family takes a mature and realistic view toward the patient and his condition, one would presume that there are possibilities of a healthy adjustment to loss.

The basic attitude of the family toward death itself is also revealed in this time of the ministry to the dying. They will demonstrate by their attitudes and actions whether they are fearful and resentful of the reality of death and are attempting to evade it or whether they accept the inevitability of this event and are seeking to adjust to it. They will indicate the degree of their understanding that death severs the relationships of life and requires a new integration. Observations such as these will enable the minister to recognize where the mourning process must begin in order to bring about a satisfactory adjustment.

The ministry to the dying, the prefuneral calls, the funeral itself, are in reality precounseling contacts with the bereaved. They pave the way for a more continuous and well-structured counseling relationship after the funeral.

Postfuneral Calls

This interpretation of the personal function of the funeral requires a continuing pastoral relationship after the funeral. It is reasonable to suggest that if the funeral is to establish a climate for mourning, the pastor has the responsibility to assist that process as it moves along through the days and weeks which follow the funeral. In his pastoral care of the bereaved after the funeral the minister has the opportunity to translate into action what he has said in the funeral service.

This is really an ethical issue. Merely to conduct the funeral services and to pay no further attention to the bereaved is sheer professionalism in the worst sense of the word. It can easily degenerate into a sort of sophisticated witch doctoring, where the pastor is called in "to say a few words" over the body, to appease the spirits, and then picks up the sack of meal which is his due and goes home. But to carry on a close pastoral relationship with the mourners for several weeks or months after the funeral is a real witness to the Christian concern and to the communion of saints.

The calls which the minister makes after the funeral can be extremely productive for a number of reasons. In the first place they are beginning to build upon the foundation which was laid during the prefuneral calls and the funeral itself. There are basic attitudes available to the mourners for their guidance in the therapeutic process. Then, too, these calls are more effective because after the funeral the bereaved can be more unhurried in his conversations. There is less pressure of activity. The prefuneral calls often cannot achieve relaxed conditions because there are many arrangements to be made, interruptions by other callers, a general state of confusion. But once the funeral is over and the daily routine begins to settle down, there is time for extended, unhurried conversations. In addition to this the postfuneral calls are usually more productive because the high emotional level which was reached before the funeral gradually recedes. It is impossible to counsel with someone who is in an extremely agitated, highly emotional state. At such a time one can only demonstrate an attitude which will open the door to counseling when the level of emotion diminishes. There is usually a gradual decline of emotion during the postfuneral period, which enables the bereaved to gain insight and perspective through counseling.

The fact that the postfuneral ministry to the mourners is so much more effective than the prefuneral pastoral care in no way deprecates the work which the pastor does with the bereaved before the funeral and in the funeral. Indeed pastoral counseling after the funeral would be most difficult if it were not for the groundwork which was laid during the earlier stages of mourning.

The purposes of the postfuneral calls are not unlike those for prefuneral pastoral care: the development of rapport and assistance in the mourning process.

The growth of rapport is necessary for effective counseling. Pastoral care cannot proceed without trust, and trust is engendered by attitudes of helpfulness and concern. The willingness of the pastor to take time in his busy schedule to make a number of calls on the bereaved signifies his interest in them and brings an openness to their relationship which will not come in a perfunctory type of pastoral care. The number and frequency of the visits will depend a good deal upon the individual situation, but it is apparent that one call will not suffice. The pastor will probably find that several calls closely following the funeral will bring out significant material which can form the basis for several more structured interviews on an appointment basis.

Some pastors are finding this program effective. Very shortly after the funeral they call in the house of mourning and give the family a copy of the funeral sermon or the entire funeral service. This serves to establish continuity between the funeral and the postfuneral pastoral care. It gives the family an opportunity to reflect upon the things which were said at the funeral and to see them more clearly in the context of their own situation. Then a few days later the pastor calls again. If the feelings which the mourners express indicate problems in adjustment, or if a discussion of the funeral service brings up questions which require further explanation, the pastor can pin-point these difficulties by saying, for example, "I take it that you're having some difficulty thinking through the question of why the God of goodness and love permits such a tragic event to happen. Would you like to come to the study on Thursday afternoon so we can take an hour or so to talk it over?" Of course this is not a set pattern, but it indicates the way in which the process can be followed out.

We have already moved into the second purpose of the postfuneral calls: assistance in the mourning process. This includes several aspects: further discussion of memories of the deceased, insight and perspective into the meaning of the mourner's loss, release from emotional tensions, a more complete understanding and interpretation of the Christian view of death and resurrection.

The need for talking over memories of the deceased is made apparent by the psychological studies of the grief reaction. Not only does it give an opportunity for the mourners to express their feelings toward the deceased, but it also is an integral part of mourning. It aids in dispelling tendencies to avoid thinking of the loss which has been sustained and points up the necessity for readjustment of life without the presence of the one who has died. The pattern of freeness and openness for these thoughts which was established in the funeral is now continued.

In most situations it is not too difficult for people to talk about their loss. But during the postfuneral calls the pastor should be careful to give ample opportunity for the mourners to discuss what their loss means to them. This provides an occasion for gaining insight and understanding into what the loss involves in their own experience. They will be helped to see the way in which their lives have disintegrated through the loss of opportunity for interaction with the deceased and will become conscious of the necessity of reintegration by forming new relationships and interests. However, the pastor must be well aware of the danger of too rapid progress in this direction. It is possible that activities which look on the surface like steps toward reintegration can actually be disintegrating factors. The crucial question is this: Are the moves to form new relationships and to work at new interests designed to keep the mourner from thinking about his loss, or are they definite attempts to integrate life once the loss of interaction with the deceased is fully realized? Too often people hinder adjustment by plunging into a frenzy of activity shortly after the funeral to take their minds off their sorrow over loss. If this is a means of escape, which it often is, it will work more for harm than help. The loss must be apprehended before the therapeutic work of reintegration can take place.

The pastor plays an important part in this reintegration. The relationship which he establishes with the mourner supports and sustains the bereaved in the face of devastating loneliness. This is not to say that he deliberately begins to fill the vacant place which has been left by the deceased, but the warmth of his concern represents the way in which new relationships can be helpful. Whenever one deals with the supportive role of the counselor, one runs a great risk of misunderstanding. The fact that the minister supports the mourners in their loss does not mean that he becomes a crutch on which they lean, making decisions for them, problem solving, making them utterly dependent upon him. This will only encourage a tendency to escape. His support comes through the assurance which his actions and attitudes give that he understands the mourner and his needs, that he is vitally concerned with helping him. This is particularly essential during the early phases of the grief reaction.

Another purpose of the postfuneral pastoral care is the release of emotional tension. The strong feelings which are present in bereavement create inner tensions which demand release. The pastor will do the mourner a great service by providing the occasion for such release. This is done through his understanding acceptance of the feelings which the mourner expresses. The mourner must feel free to talk, to pour out his story without embarrassment or the fear of criticism. The pastoral counselor will make no effort to detour any expressions of strong emotion—weeping, anger, bitterness. Where strong guilt feelings have been manifested, the pastor will accept the confession of the mourner without judging him. This is very difficult to do. It can be accomplished only if the pastor realizes that confession is a means of releasing the burden of guilt and should not be taken as an occasion for complicating the sense of guilt by passing judgment on what the parishioner has felt or done. The free, accepting, and understanding nature which the pastor demonstrated in the funeral is put to the practical test in the postfuneral ministry to the bereaved.

The postfuneral ministry also offers the possibility of helping the mourner to a deeper understanding of the Christian view of death and resurrection. As the level of emotion goes down, it is possible to approach the subject more on an intellectual level. While the mourners are under powerful emotional tension, such an undertaking is quite in vain. It is only after they are able to transcend their personal crisis, having found perspective on their loss, that they are able to view the subject of an intellectual understanding of death and resurrection and think it through in terms of their own situation. The Christian faith is then experienced in existential reality.

Although to my knowledge it has seldom been attempted, there are very real possibilities for improving our ministry to the bereaved through the techniques of group therapy. This would be particularly applicable in the larger parishes where a pastor could not possibly give enough time to each of the houses of mourning

to which he is called to work through the mourning adjustment
with his parishioners. In such a situation after several personal
calls in the home the bereaved could be invited to a group session
of folk in the same situation of bereavement. There under the direct-
tion of a trained leader they could explore their grief reactions together and reach an adjustment through mutual assistance. The
relationships which would be formed within the group would
make a valuable contribution to reintegration. However, the leader would have to be well aware of the danger of relationships of
dependence rather than support being formed within the group.
This group approach would be a most fruitful field for further
investigation and experimentation.

Pastoral Care of Strangers to the Church

Every minister comes into contact with a number of situations
where he is called upon for a funeral ministry to families which
are strangers to the church. The question arises. Can one conduct a
funeral effectively for someone who is a stranger? Naturally it
would be much more difficult to minister to the needs of people
whom one does not know, but it is not impossible. In such situations
the arrangements for the funeral are often very impersonal, most
frequently being made through the undertaker. But the minister
can make them personal by immediately taking the opportunity to
visit the bereaved, calling upon them before and after the funeral.
His lack of knowledge of their background will be some handicap,
but the possibility of understanding and accepting the feelings
which they express is not reduced. In such cases the therapy of
the funeral service itself assumes even greater importance than
under ordinary circumstances, because it is the one certain contact
which the pastor will have with the bereaved. If the funeral service
and the calls of the pastor demonstrate his concern, the way is
opened for an effective pastoral relationship even with strangers
and the unchurched.

The funeral conducted for the unchurched is a real evangelistic
opportunity. However, the outreach of the church will not be
served by the pastor who uses such a funeral for exhortation or

censure, but by the minister who manifests a genuine concern for the needs of the bereaved both in the funeral service and in the pastoral care which he offers to them before and after the funeral.

Pastoral care of the bereaved and the funeral form an interrelated unit in the total work of the pastor and the ministry of the church. Their effectiveness will be greatly impaired if they do not fit together into a pattern of consistency in theory and practice.

CHAPTER NINE

THE FUNERAL AND THE TOTAL MINISTRY
OF THE CHURCH

THE FUNERAL is not an isolated event in the ministry of the church to the needs of its people. Binding up the brokenhearted is but one of the many functions which the church has continued to perform throughout the centuries as a part of its total responsibility and mission. The funeral cannot be lifted out and reshaped without some concommitant reformation of the church itself.

It is undeniable that that which affects a part of the whole affects the totality as well. The experience of many men who have undertaken graduate study in pastoral care supports the validity of this process. Their labors in the parish convinced them of their inadequacy in meeting many of the situations which were presented when parishioners sought counseling. As this conviction grew, they sought additional training in the counseling ministry. Many of them went back to school or into clinical training to learn a technique which would enable them to be better counselors. But they found, as their work progressed, that they were learning much more than a technique; they were developing a pastoral theology. They found upon completing their training that they were in possession of a consistent philosophical and theological framework for the applications of the techniques which they had come to learn. They discovered that their preaching, their teaching, their organizational and administrative work, had been radically affected by what they learned of counseling. That which changes a part of the whole does change the totality as well.

If this is true, the changes which have been proposed for rethinking the purpose of the funeral also have far-reaching ramifications for the church and the ministry. The techniques which are employed to stress the personal function of the funeral have a bearing upon the total picture of the work of the church.

Let us see, then, how this interpretation and analysis of the funeral carries with it a number of implications, not only for the funeral service, but also for the church and the minister.

Implications for the Church

In theory the work of the church is always related to human needs. In practice this relationship is sometimes overlooked. There have been times in the history of the church when its whole activity has been polemic or defensive. Dogmatism in theology and authoritarianism in ethics have been ways in which the church has sought to protect the institution against those things which it considered antagonists.

It is possible to see church history operating in cyclical fashion. The primitive church was a sect. It was intent upon its mission to spread the gospel in obedience to the great commission of the Lord of the church. Although it was under scrutiny and attack by various political and religious forces, its genius reposed in the concern which it had for the world and for the members of the fellowship. The needs of the individual, both physical and spiritual, were focal in its concern. But under the continuing pressure of persecution and the rise of the heresies, the church began erecting protective walls about it. It became an institution which had to be defended. Apologetics became polemics; conformity to dogma and submission to authority became major protective devices. Under such circumstances the needs of the individual were sublimated, and the needs of the institution became the primary concern.

Then a new sect would break off from the established church, as in the Reformation. Once again there was a new vitality, a new concern for individual needs. The mutuality of the early church was revived. But soon the sect would settle into orthodoxy and institutionalism. The church once again viewed its mission as protecting the institution rather than heeding the individual needs of members of the fellowship. This pattern occurred again and again. Only when the church does not feel a compulsive need to defend

itself, can it devote its full attention to meeting the needs of the
flock for which it is responsible.

A great many of the proposals for reconsideration of the funeral
have been essentially defensive or protective moves on the part of
the church. They have been designed to win people for the church,
to force acceptance of the Christian assumptions about the meaning
of death, to urge submission to an acceptable pattern of behavior
in bereavement.

When we examine the personal function of the funeral, we see
that the primary concern must be the need of the individual
mourner. The funeral is more than just a ritual which encourages
people to depend upon the church, or even upon Christianity, in a
time of crisis. The funeral is a way of helping them. The mission
of the church is to serve them in their need rather than to serve
itself. The funeral is not only a way of praising and glorifying God,
as some authors have said; it is also a way of confronting and meeting human needs.

Some people may object to the question I have raised about the
appropriateness of certain passages from the Scripture for use in
the funeral service. Others may take issue with the way in which
I have supported some of the practices which reformers of the
funeral have been trying to dispose of. Still others may suggest that
I have done violence to the Christian interpretation of death by
placing some emphasis upon the physical. To those I would have to
reply that my proposals have been based upon the meeting of
human needs in the time of bereavement.

Until such needs are met, the individual will experience real
difficulty in coming to a meaningful understanding of the purpose
of the church and his place in it, the meaning of Christian theology
and its relevance for his life. The churches learned this lesson at the
close of World War II. Much of the world was in great need,
physical and spiritual. Vast sums of money were raised by American churches for world relief. How was the money expended? Was
it given first to build churches or send missionaries, important
though that might have been? No, it was invested in food and
clothing. The church reasoned wisely that until stomachs had

something in them and bodies were warmed, it would be difficult to bring the message of reconciliation. In fact the church recognized that by feeding the hungry and clothing the naked it was preaching the message of reconciliation. The funeral can be looked upon in the same way. Can we expect those who are hungry for comfort and peace of mind to find solace only in an explanation of the Christian understanding of death, even though it be true? Is it not far more reasonable to suppose that by meeting their need for comfort, by enabling them to mourn with the full resources of the Christian faith to aid them, they will come to a fuller understanding of Christian faith and hope? Faith is not merely intellectual acceptance apart from a rootage in the experience of the believer.

Many of the ceremonies and rites of the church have become devoid of meaning to people because of their lack of concern with human needs. If they are allowed to become rites which are performed only for the sake of themselves, without due recognition of individual needs and an effort to meet those needs, they can hardly be expected to become significant events in the movement of the spirit of God into the lives of men.

This study implies that unless the personal function of the rites of the church is consciously considered and acted upon, an effective means for the working of the grace of God is circumvented.

Implications for the Ministry

There are also implications in this evaluation of the funeral for the minister and his work. The therapeutic process in cases of bereavement is determined in a large part by the pastor's attitude as manifested in the funeral service, since this is the one inevitable contact the pastor has with the bereaved. His attitude in the presence of the bereaved, his manner in conducting the services, his integrity and self-possession, have an important bearing upon the therapeutic effect of the funeral. Although we would not want to push this point to extremity, we must admit that the way in which something is said may make a more helpful impression on the mourners than what is said. An understanding manner is a requisite for a therapeutic funeral, no matter how carefully it is prepared.

The traditional function of the pastor is manifold. He is the leader of the congregation, employed by the church to be an administrator, a preacher, a teacher, a counselor, and a representative of the church in society. He is the leader of worship in the church. It is his responsibility to conduct the services and rites of the church for the benefit of the congregation and the community. In addition to this he is a shepherd, not in the sense of one who drives the flock to do this or that, but as one who cares for and watches over the sheep.

All these functions or roles are involved when a minister is called upon to conduct a funeral. He preaches, teaches, leads the worship, counsels, and cares for the flock, all in this one activity. This is true no matter how one views the funeral.

However, when we consider the essential character of the personal function of the funeral, the role of the minister in the funeral assumes even greater importance. If the funeral is to be of help in enabling individuals to mourn and find comfort, the task of the minister is not an easy one. It requires that he must get far beyond the detached professionalism which has crept into so much pastoral work. The pastor cannot content himself with a brief interview with the bereaved family before the funeral, a shoddily prepared funeral service, and a perfunctory pastoral call after the funeral.

In order to meet human needs in the funeral, the pastor must be sensitive to the needs of men's lives. He will have to become familiar with the dynamic forces which operate within the grief reaction, seeing these forces at work in the experience of the people to whom he ministers. It will be necessary for the minister to become familiar with the data which have been presented by psychological research on the subject of the grief reaction and the recent books on pastoral counseling. The mere fact that he has a love for people is not enough. It must be accompanied by some knowledge of the motivations and causes which underlie human behavior.

Coupled with this sensitivity to the dynamics of individual be-havior there must be an ability to evaluate. In a sense this is simi-lar to the diagnostic work of the physician. In his dealings with the bereaved family the pastor needs not only a sensitivity to their needs but also an ability to understand and evaluate these needs. Naturally it is impossible for the average pastor to possess the acumen of a skilled psychiatrist in seeing the meaning of all the feelings and experiences of his parishioners. This does not mean that he cannot function as a pastoral counselor, or that he cannot attempt to minister to human needs, psychologically interpreted, in the funeral.

These implications, which I have been discussing, have to do largely with the knowledge and capacity for understanding needed for an effective ministry to the bereaved. We see that an applica-tion of the principles which affirm the personal function of the funeral involves more than the learning of a technique. It entails the working out of an integrated theological and philosophical view of man, which will affect all aspects of the minister's work.

So many attempts to reform the funeral have placed their em-phasis almost completely on changing parishioners and their atti-tudes toward funeral practices. Very often ministers have been very frustrated, because they have found that they were resisting tra-ditions which were the accrual of the experience of several genera-tions. They were then faced with the dilemma of capitulating to custom or imposing their wishes upon the community in an authori-tarian manner.

The approach to the funeral which is made in this book is directed primarily at the pastor, suggesting that he rethink his whole at-titude toward the funeral and pastoral care of the bereaved, and that he make a thorough evaluation of his work. The primary changes are to be wrought in the pastor. As his ministry in bereave-ment changes its emphasis and intent, the attitudes of people to-ward those elements of the funeral ritual and practices will also change. Since the needs of the mourners are always held to be paramount, without any intrusion of vested interest on the part of the church or the minister, parishioners are gradually brought to the understanding that changes are being made to help them to mourn.

There is another way in which the work of the pastor has bearing upon bereavement. It is possible for the minister to do a great deal in utilizing nonfuneral occasions to bring an intepretation of death, bereavement, and mourning to his people. The Episcopal Church provides such an opportunity in the celebration of All Souls' Day. Some churches of Lutheran background observe Memorial Sunday (*Totenfest*) on the Sunday before Advent. Although these are occasions for honoring the memory of those who have died during the year, they also present an excellent opportunity to preach an objective sermon on the meaning of death and the place of mourning.

Pastors also might urge organizations to devote a meeting to a discussion of the subject. Articles in church papers and books on the subject in the church library are effective means of stimulating people to think seriously on the meaning of the therapy of mourning before they are called upon to mourn. The wise pastor will seek to educate his people to deal with grief properly before they have the experience of grief.

These are some of the implications which this view of the funeral has for various aspects of the pastor's work.

Implications for the Future of the Funeral

The future of the funeral does not hinge upon the question of the survival of this rite but on the question of performance. There is something so instinctive about a ceremonial accompaniment to death that the continuation of the funeral is not doubtful. But the future of the funeral in terms of usefulness versus unthinking acceptance of custom does hang in the balance. We feel no constraint to work for the continued existence of the funeral; this will take care of itself. Our concern is to promote the usefulness and relevance of the funeral in the mourning situation, making it an agency of maximum aid and comfort to the mourners.

This study of the funeral and pastoral care is based upon the supposition that the modern funeral is not adequately meeting the needs of those who mourn. This assumption is supported by several observations on contemporary funerals.

In the first place, there appears to be a heavy reliance upon stereotyped forms in conducting the funeral. Many pastors, either by church custom or preference, plan their services almost entirely on the basis of a prepared order. Whatever variation is introduced is made largely to avoid repetition. As a result the funeral is in danger of becoming static, undynamic, lacking a vital relationship to the realities of life.

A second very similar type of inadequacy is seen in a "mass production" method of conducting funerals, where a pastor produces the same funeral over and over as the demand arises. This is not limited solely to those churches which average several funerals a week. It can take place in the ministry of any church. It is a result of a basic insensitivity on the part of the pastor toward the mourners. This does not mean that he is unfeeling or unsympathetic toward them. But it does indicate that he lacks understanding of their individual situation. He is not sufficiently conscious of the needs of the individuals involved to take adequate steps in the funeral to meet these needs. In truth such a pattern is symptomatic of the poverty of the pastor's view of an individual personality. His whole view of man is reflected in the insensitivity of his funeral ministry. If he truly appreciated the unique dignity of each individual, he would demonstrate this understanding by rejecting a standard funeral in favor of a service which recognized and ministered to the needs of these particular individual mourners.

The third inadequacy of the modern funeral comes about through a misunderstanding of the therapy of mourning. By failing to familiarize himself with the psychological data regarding bereavement, by resisting the *rapprochement* between psychology and religion, the pastor may conduct funerals in a way which will move at cross purposes in meeting the psychological needs of mourners. Without an understanding that mourning is a therapeutic process the funeral may seek to bring comfort by avoiding the painful experience of mourning. The Christian faith may be presented as a way of circumventing mourning rather than as a resource which enables the Christian to mourn and be healed.

Because of these inadequacies I have proposed the concept of the personal function of the funeral. In this way the funeral can be seen as a means for ministering to the needs of the individual mourners. It becomes more than just another service of the church or the performance of a ritual because death has occurred. The understanding of the personal function of the funeral in no way detracts from the element of worship which is present in the service, nor does it say that the funeral is purely subjective. It does, however, propose that meeting the needs of the particular mourning situation is an essential part of every funeral.

The proper carrying out of the personal function of the funeral points the way to the correcting of those points at which the funeral is inadequately fulfilling its purpose. Instead of a stereotyped following of an established order without due regard for the variable elements of the individual situation, the understanding of the personal function of the funeral calls for a degree of flexibility which permits the development of the service in accordance with the need of the mourners. The same thing is true of the opposition which an understanding of the personal function of the funeral offers to an insensitive "mass production." The mere feeling of sympathy must be augmented with an empathetic understanding of the mourners. Once this is done, it is virtually inevitable that the pastor will see the funeral as a unique opportunity to minister to particular needs. The understanding of the personal function of the funeral also carries with it the demand for a proper appraisal of the work of mourning. Based on a sound psychological foundation, in addition to the theological and cultural structure, the funeral assumes a new importance for the ministry in bereavement. Here the close alliance of the funeral with pastoral care is seen. The two cannot be divorced. They are integral parts of the process by which the minister, as representative of the church and servant of the Word, can be of help to the brokenhearted.

In order to bring about an emphasis on the personal function of the funeral, I have taken issue with some of the common funeral forms and practices of our time. This is not done in the spirit of iconoclasm but as a corrective measure to ameliorate the work of the minister in grief situations. I have also supported as valuable some of the practices which are being challenged on various fronts in the life of the church. I have been willing to cut across the currents of some of the efforts to reform the funeral because I make the personal function of the funeral a primary concern. I am, therefore, unwilling to subjugate the satisfaction of human needs to purely aesthetic or liturgical considerations. The funeral, I believe, was made for man, not man for the funeral.

Throughout the centuries the church has accepted the responsibility to respond to the cries of those who are in need. Never has it ceased its exploration of new and better ways to serve. Therefore we are justified in the hope that a critical evaluation of the ministry to the bereaved will enable the church to lead its people to a fuller integration of their lives.

BIBLIOGRAPHY

Books

Blackwood, Andrew W. *The Funeral*. Philadelphia: Westminster Press, 1942. A source book for understanding the mechanics of the funeral, especially helpful for the inexperienced pastor; a discussion of the funeral from the standpoint of the ceremony rather than a dynamic understanding of the individuals involved.

Cabot, Richard C., and Dicks, Russell L. *The Art of Ministering to the Sick*. New York: Macmillan Co., 1947. Still one of the outstanding volumes on pastoral work with the sick, with a helpful chapter on ministering to the bereaved.

Fromm, Erich. *Man for Himself*. New York: Rinehart & Co., Inc., 1947. A psychological interpretation of ethics which has special bearing upon the way in which cultural pressure impinges upon the individual.

Grinker, Roy R., and Spiegel, John P. *Men under Stress*. Philadelphia: Blakiston Co., 1945. A study of the reactions of U.S.A.F. men in combat during World War II, giving helpful information on the effect of bereavement due to loss of crew members.

Halsey, Jesse. *A Living Hope*. New York: Abingdon Press, 1932. A loose-leaf compilation of funeral resource materials for selective use.

Harmon, Nolan B., Jr. *The Pastor's Ideal Funeral Manual*. New York: Abingdon-Cokesbury Press, 1942. A compilation of funeral services of several denominations and a resource book of materials for funeral services.

Hiltner, Seward. *Pastoral Counseling*. New York and Nashville: Abingdon-Cokesbury Press, 1949. A book which provides the pastoral work of the minister with a sound theoretical basis and plan for operation.

————. *Self-Understanding Through Psychology and Religion*. New York: Charles Scribner's Sons, 1951. A proposal for self-acceptance through self-understanding, with a thoughtful section on bereavement and death.

Horney, Karen. *Our Inner Conflicts*. New York: W. W. Norton & Co., 1945. An interpretation of personality patterns and neuroses.

Leach, William H., ed. *The Cokesbury Funeral Manual*. Nashville: Cokesbury Press, 1932. A widely used nondenominational resource book for funerals.

McNeill, John T. *A History of the Cure of Souls*. New York: Harper &

Bros., 1951. A broad and detailed historical survey of pastoral ministrations, limited largely to a consideration of pastoral guidance and disciplinary regulation rather than pastoral care in the modern understanding.

Morrison, James Dalton, ed. *Minister's Service Book*. Chicago: Willett, Clark & Co., 1937. A nondenominational resource book for church worship.

Rogers, William F. *Ye Shall Be Comforted*. Philadelphia: Westminster Press, 1950. An excellent interpretation of the modern psychological knowledge of grief and bereavement and the way in which the resources of Christianity have bearing upon mourning.

Smith, W. Halsey, ed. *A Service Book*. Chicago: National Selected Morticians, 1925. A nondenominational resource book for funeral services.

Wallis, Charles L., ed. *The Funeral Encyclopedia*. New York: Harper & Bros., 1953. A collection of funeral resources and sermons.

Wise, Carroll A. *Pastoral Counseling: Its Theory and Practice*. New York: Harper & Bros., 1951. A good basic volume on the theory of pastoral counseling, with a very good section in the last chapter on counseling the bereaved.

Book of Church Order, The. The service book of the Presbyterian Church in the U.S.

Book of Common Prayer, The. The prayer and service book of the Protestant Episcopal Church in the U.S.A.

Book of Common Worship, The. The service book of the Presbyterian Church in the U.S.A.

Book of Worship, The. The service book of the Evangelical and Reformed Church.

Ritual of The Methodist Church, The. The funeral service as printed in the *Discipline of The Methodist Church*.

Articles

Freud, Sigmund. "Mourning and Melancholia," *Collected Papers*. London: Hogarth Press and the Institute of Psycho-Analysis, 1948. IV, 152-70. One of the earliest studies of mourning in modern psychology.

Greer, Ina May. "Grief Must Be Faced," *The Christian Century*, Feb. 28, 1945, pp. 269-71. An excellent proposal for an attitude toward mourning which allows deep feelings to be expressed rather than repressed.

Lindemann, Erich. "Symptomatology and Management of Acute Grief," *The American Journal of Psychiatry*, CI (Sept., 1944), 141-49. The outstanding modern contribution to the study of grief and bereavement, the basis for most contemparary work in this field.

Middaugh, Bruce L. "The Ministry of Bereavement." *The Pastor*, July, 1948, pp. 10-11. A brief presentation of the function of the minister in counseling the bereaved and in offering the resources of the Christian faith to them.

Schachtel, Ernest G. "On Memory and Childhood Amnesia," *A Study of Interpersonal Relations*, ed. Patrick Mullahy, New York: Hermitage Press, Inc., 1949. An interesting chapter which has particular bearing on the subject of mourning in its material on the way in which memories are recalled.

Sherrill, Helen H., and Lewis J. "Interpreting Death to Children," *The International Journal of Religious Education*, Oct., 1951, pp. 4-6. An article on the meaning of death which will be especially helpful for pastors and parents. It has been reprinted in pamphlet form by the National Council of the Churches of Christ in the United States of America, 79 East Adams Street, Chicago 3, Ill.

Stern, Karl, Williams, Gwendolyn M., and Prados, Miguel. "Grief Reactions in Later Life," *The American Journal of Psychiatry*, CIIX (1951), 289-93. A study of interpersonal relations of twenty-five persons in later life who were suffering from grief reactions.

Vogt, Von Ogden. "We Commit This Body." *The Christian Century*, Mar. 21, 1945, pp. 362-63. A defense of the funeral service versus the memorial service, which draws some excellent implications on the meaning of the body for the bereaved.

Unpublished Material

Applebee, W. Thomas. "When Death Comes." A booklet for distribution in the Community Congregational Church of Condon, Ore.

"Funerals in the Light of Our Knowledge of Grief and Bereavement." Summarized Report of Joint Session of May 5, 1950, Department of Pastoral Services, Commission on Religion and Health, Federal Council of Churches of Christ in America.

Messersmith, Lauren Harry. "The Minister's Relation to the Funeral." Unpublished Bachelor of Divinity thesis, Federated Theological Faculty, University of Chicago, 1945.

INDEX